The Rainforest

Rainforests are jungles filled with tall, densely growing, evergreen trees. They occur in areas with high yearly rainfall. Most are along the equator.

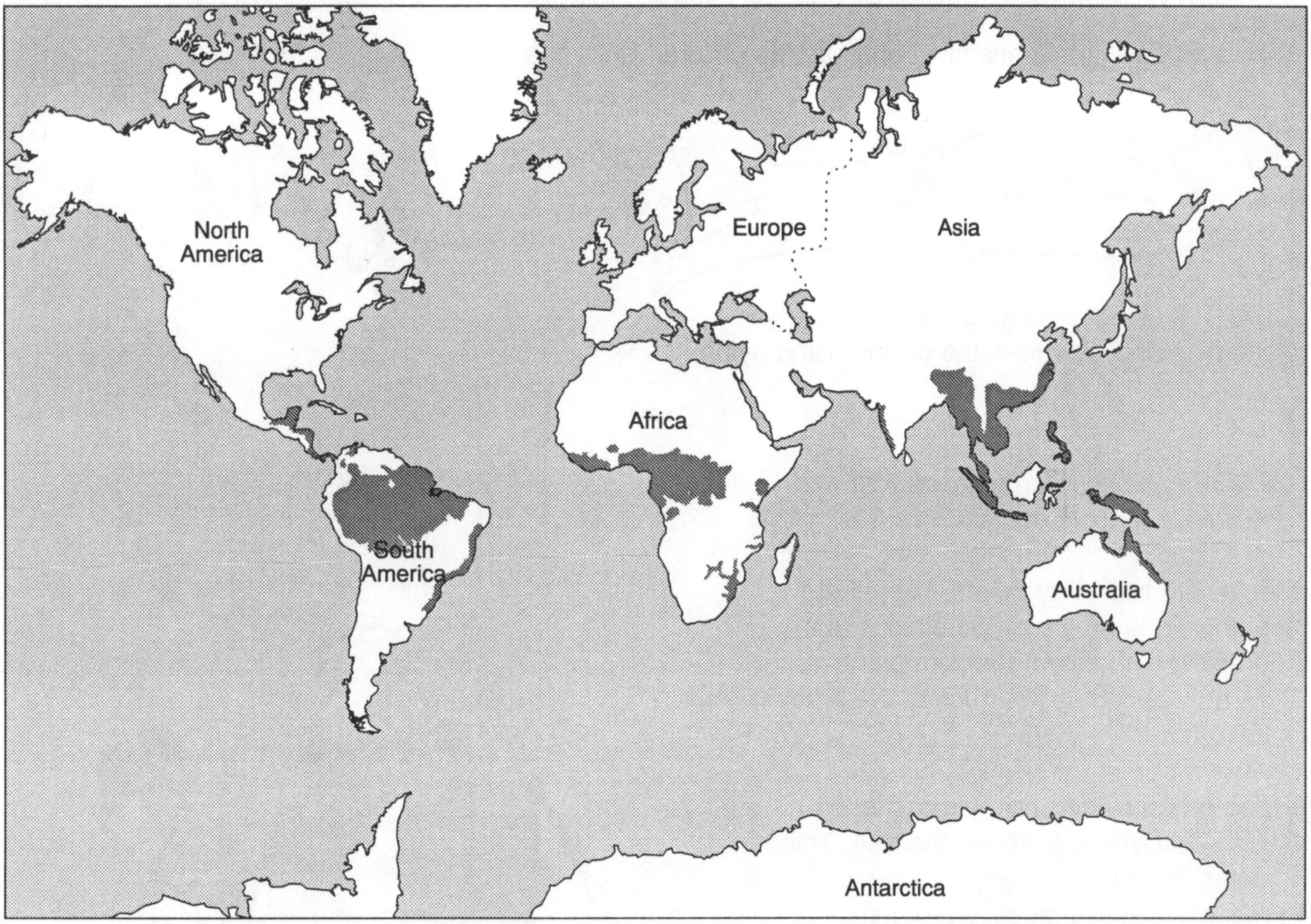

Questions to ask:

- What does the rainforest look like?
- What is found in the rainforest?
- How is the rainforest being hurt today?
- Where do the animals in the rainforest live?

Resources:

Provide books that have colorful pictures to give students a sense of how the rainforest and its wildlife appears.

At Home in the Rain Forest by Diane Willow; Charlesbridge, 1991.
A Walk in the Rainforest by Kristin Joy Pratt; Dawn Publications, 1992.
Jungles by Mark J. Rauzon; Doubleday, 1992.
Rain Forest Rap available through the World Wildlife Fund.

Your Room Design

It is very important to create a learning environment which enhances the theme being taught. Begin a new unit on a Monday so that you have the weekend to get the room ready. When the children walk into the room, they should be stepping into a "rainforest." The tropical rainforest is a place of beauty and awe. The following ideas will help you transform your room into an environment the children will enjoy.

Play a tape of jungle animal sounds as the children enter the room.

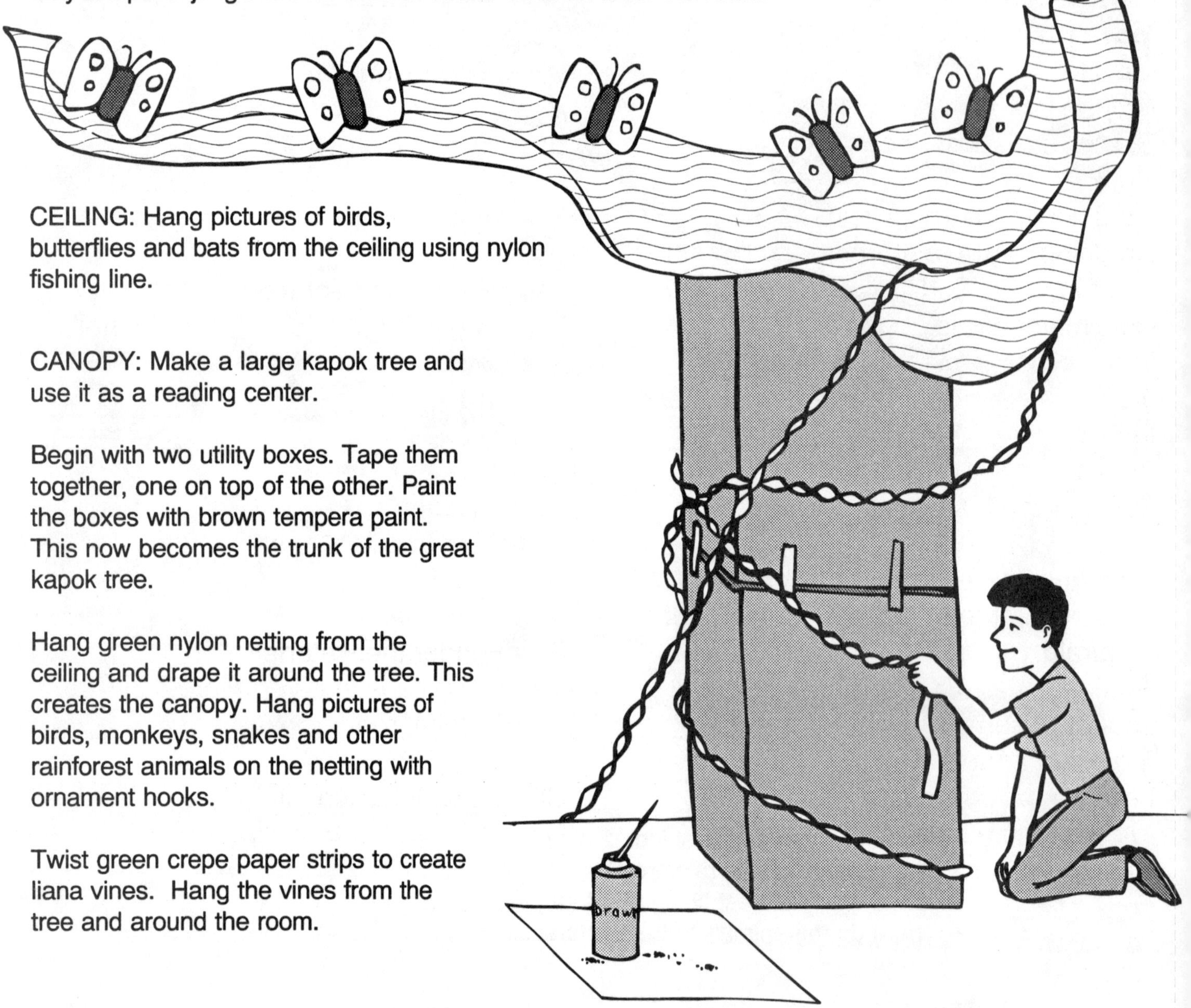

CEILING: Hang pictures of birds, butterflies and bats from the ceiling using nylon fishing line.

CANOPY: Make a large kapok tree and use it as a reading center.

Begin with two utility boxes. Tape them together, one on top of the other. Paint the boxes with brown tempera paint. This now becomes the trunk of the great kapok tree.

Hang green nylon netting from the ceiling and drape it around the tree. This creates the canopy. Hang pictures of birds, monkeys, snakes and other rainforest animals on the netting with ornament hooks.

Twist green crepe paper strips to create liana vines. Hang the vines from the tree and around the room.

WINDOWS: Paint a large mural on the windows of the room. Mix a small amount of liquid soap with tempera paint. Paint plants, animals and flowers found in the rainforest.

DOOR: Cover the door with green paper. Make a sign reading,

Welcome to the Rainforest.

Note: The teacher stands in front of the children who repeat and follow the actions of the teacher.

Walk through the Rainforest

Let's take a walk through the rainforest.
Are you ready?
I see a trail.
(point your finger)
Let's follow the trail.
(slap thighs to make walking sounds)
Stomp, stomp, stomp, stomp.

I'm going in the rainforest.
I'm going in the rainforest, and I'm not afraid.
No, I'm not afraid.
Look, a vine.
(point your finger)
Let's swing on the vine.
(move arms as if swinging on a vine)
Swing, swing, swing, swing.

I'm going in the rainforest.
I'm going in the rainforest, and I'm not afraid.
No, I'm not afraid.
Look, a mountain!
(point your finger)
Let's climb the mountain.
(move arms and legs as if climbing)
Climb, climb, climb, climb.

I'm going in the rainforest.
I'm going in the rainforest, and I'm not afraid.
Look, a waterfall!
(point your finger)
Let's swim under the waterfall.
(make swimming motions with arms)
Swim, swim, swim, swim.

I'm going in the rainforest.
I'm going in the rainforest, and I'm not afraid.
No, I'm not afraid.
Look, I see a gorilla!
(point your finger)
Let's feed him bananas.
(make motions of peeling a banana)
Peel, peel, peel, peel.

I'm going in the rainforest.
I'm going in the rainforest, and I'm not afraid.
Look, another vine!
(point your finger)
EEK! That's not a vine.
It's a python!
(make running motions)
Run, run, run, run.

Swim under the waterfall.
(repeat motions in reverse order)
Swim, swim, swim, swim.

Climb down the mountain.
Climb, climb, climb, climb.

Swing on the vine.
Swing, swing, swing, swing.

Run up the trail.
(run in place)
Run, run, run, run.
Whew!
(wipe brow)
We're back at camp!

Layers of the Rainforest

The rainforest is a dense jungle of plants and animals. The plants are so thick that they seem to form various layers. In this unit we will be learning about four different layers: the emergent, the canopy, the understory and the forest floor. Students will learn that certain animals are especially adapted for one level but not another.

The following activity will give students experience with the names and facts about the different layers. When this activity is complete, it becomes an ideal aid in communicating your classroom curriculum with parents. Children can take this completed activity home to share with their families. It is a fine opportunity for parent and child to discuss the environmental impact of the rainforest.

Reproduce pages 5 and 6 for each student. Invite them to cut apart the sections and paste in the correct order on a sheet of 12" x 18" (30.5 x 45.7 cm) construction paper. Students may then color the illustration while you share facts with them about the various layers. Check your library or bookstore for the most recent references.

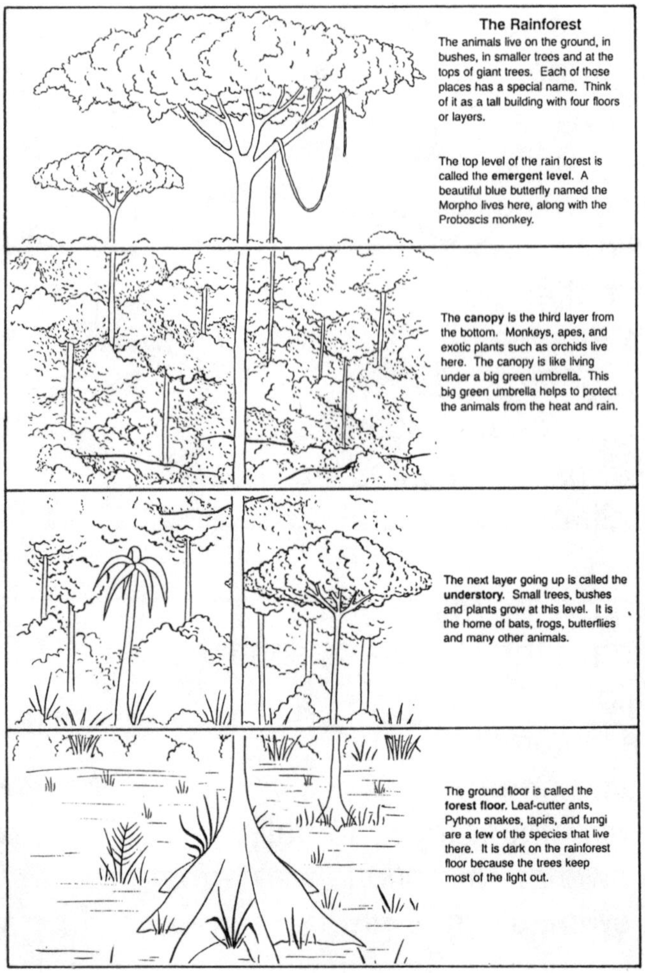

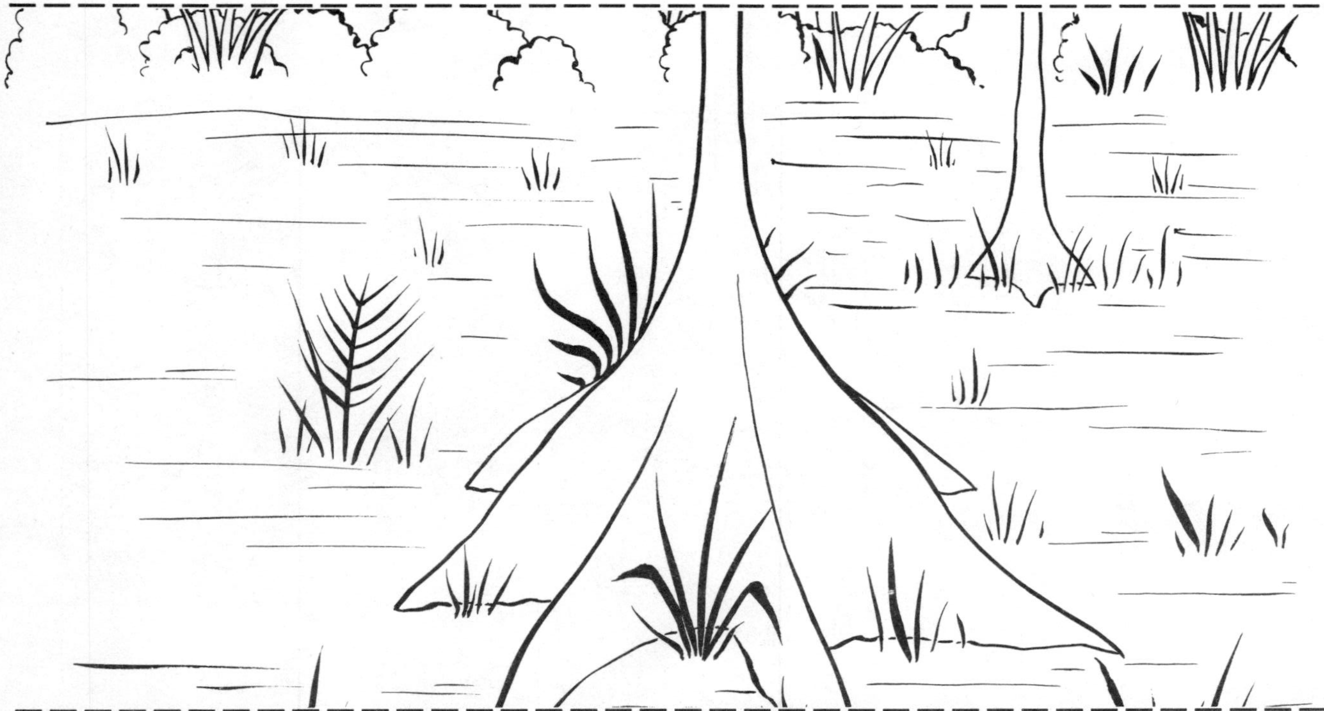

The ground floor is called the **forest floor**. Leaf-cutter ants, Python snakes, tapirs, and fungi are a few of the species that live there. It is dark on the rainforest floor because the trees keep most of the light out.

The next layer going up is called the **understory**. Small trees, bushes and plants grow at this level. It is the home of bats, frogs, butterflies and many other animals.

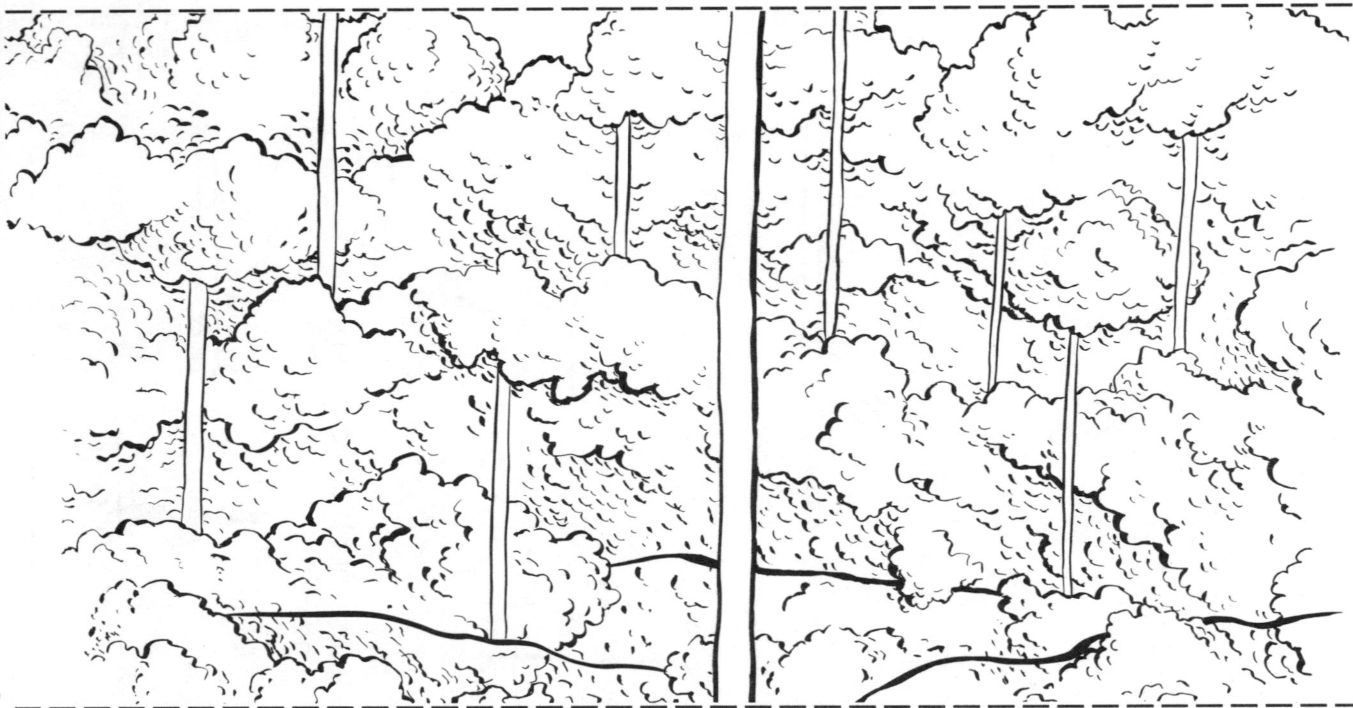

The **canopy** is the third layer from the bottom. Monkeys, apes, and exotic plants such as orchids live here. The canopy is like living under a big green umbrella. This big green umbrella helps to protect the animals from the heat and rain.

The Rainforest

The animals live on the ground, in bushes, in smaller trees and at the tops of giant trees. Each of these places has a special name. Think of it as a tall building with four floors or layers.

The top level of the rain forest is called the **emergent level**. A beautiful blue butterfly named the Morpho lives here, along with the Proboscis monkey.

Sing this song to the tune of "*If You're Happy and You Know It*"

Layers in the Forest

There are layers in the forest, yes indeed.
Yes indeed!
There are layers in the forest, yes indeed.
Yes indeed!
Emergent, canopy and the understory.
There are layers in the forest, yes indeed.
Yes indeed!

The emergent's home to birds, and butterflies.
Butterflies!
The emergent's home to birds and butterflies.
Butterflies!
The trees are so high that they almost touch the sky.
The emergent's home to birds and butterflies.
Butterflies!

The canopy is like a big umbrella.
Big umbrella!
The canopy is like a big umbrella.
Big umbrella!
Monkeys, sloths, orangutans, eat all the fruit they can.
The canopy is like a big umbrella.
Big umbrella!

The understory's home to many snakes.
Many snakes!
The understory's home to many snakes.
Many snakes!
They eat cats and bats and rats,
And they like the gnats for snacks.
The understory's home to many snakes.
Many snakes!

The forest floor is dim and dark and wet.
Dark and wet!
The forest floor is dim and dark and wet.
Dark and wet!
Oh, the ants go marching by,
As they watch the birds up high.
The forest floor is dim and dark and wet.
Dark and wet!

by Debby DePauw

Products of the Rainforest

The rainforests of Earth are extremely important to all of us, not just the people living close to them. They provide products we use. They provide homes for an enormous variety of plant and animal life. They help replenish the oxygen in our atmosphere.

We use hundreds of products from the rainforest each year. Some of the plants that grow in the rainforest are used in medicines to help save lives. If the rainforest continues to be cut down, we will lose many species of plants forever.

Many of the fruits we eat originated in the rainforest. Guavas, mangos, dates, lemons, limes, oranges, bananas, coconuts, Brazil nuts and cashews are a few of the foods grown in the rainforest.

The people who live in the rainforest tap rubber trees for latex. We use a form of latex to make gloves, stickers, shoes, and even bubble gum.

Set up a display table with products from the rainforest.

The Future

If the rainforests continue to be cut down, we will lose many species of plants forever. These forests are being cut down all over the world. In some areas the trees are harvested for the lumber they provide. In other areas they are cut to clear land for farming.

Fortunately people are becoming aware of the importance of these areas and in some places reserves are being set aside. However, it is a complex problem and much remains to be done.

Help your students become aware of what they receive from the rainforests and how they can help preserve these areas.

How do the trees in the rainforest help people?
What do we get from plants in the rainforest?
What will happen to the animals in the rainforests if too many trees are cut down?
What can we do to help save the rainforests?

Animals of the Rainforest

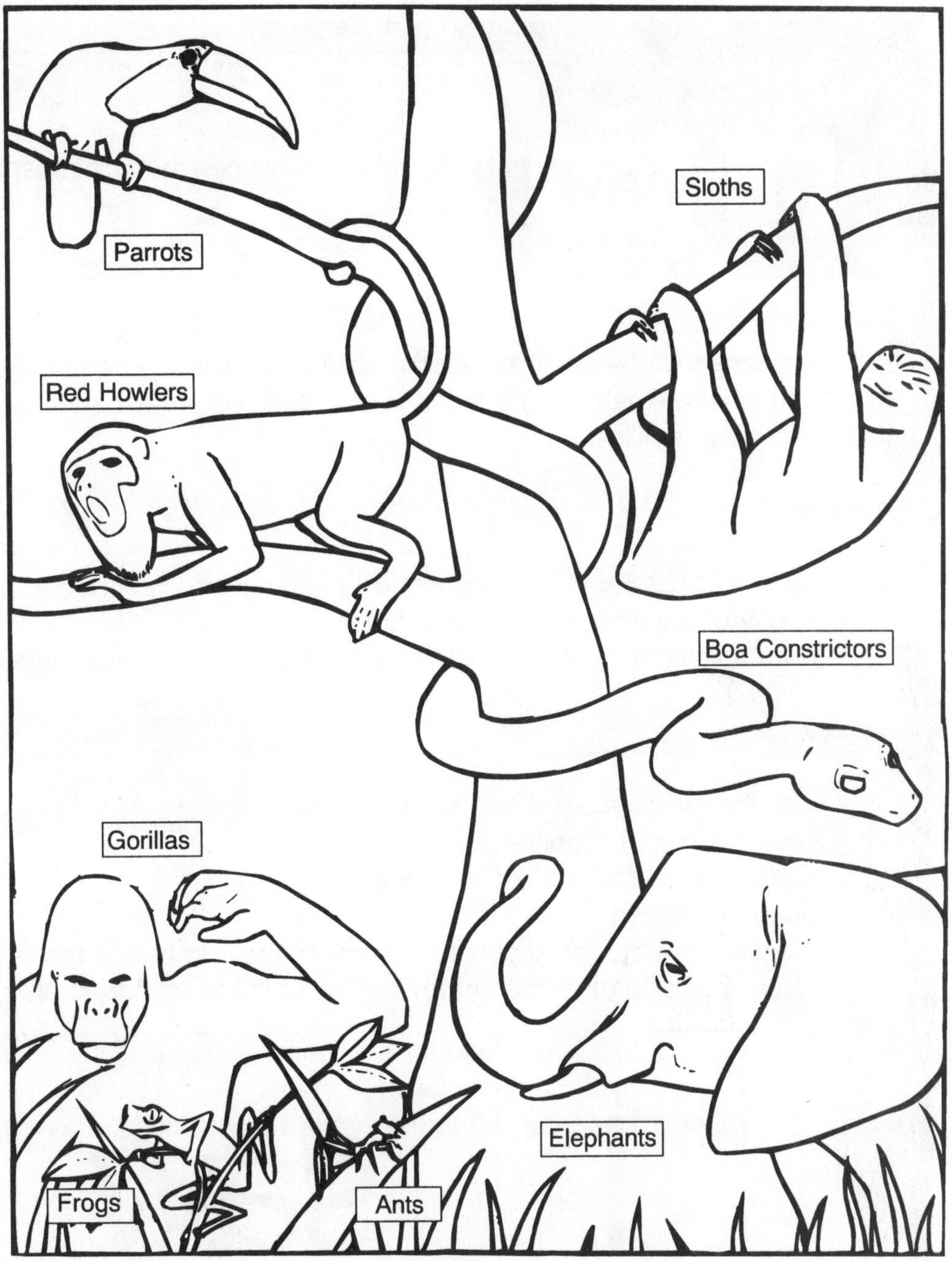

Each level of the rainforest is filled with a wide diversity of animals. Some live only in specific areas, others move freely up and down the various levels. Animals such as ants and birds exist in all rainforests in one form or another, while animals such as gorillas or tree kangaroos live only in very specific places.

Because of the lush growth of a wide variety of types of plants there is an abundance of food for plant-eating animals, which in turn provide food for the meat-eaters. Over half of all the species of animals on earth live in these rainforests and new species are being discovered every day.

In this book, your students will be learning about some general groupings of animals as well as some specific species. You will find these animals depicted on the poster that is included within this book.

Rainforest Animal Book

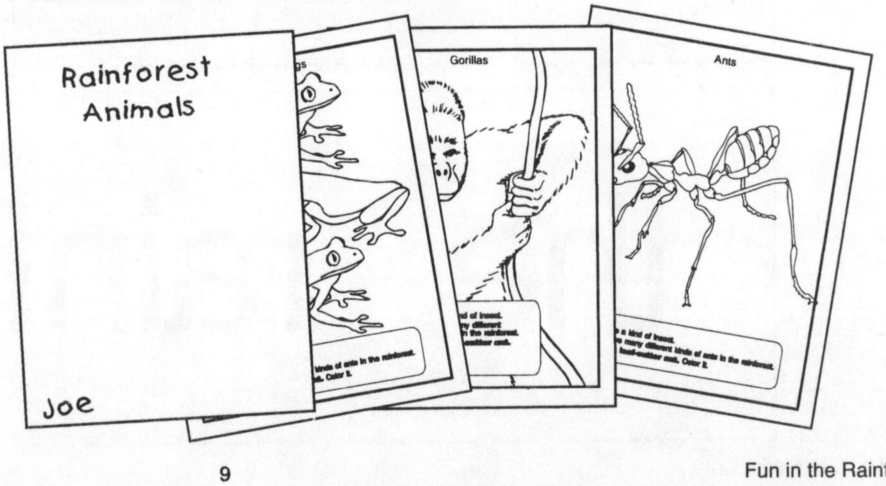

Your students can make their own Rainforest Animal Book. Save each of the starred pages in this unit. Staple these pages into a cover which the child has decorated.

My Own Book about Animals of the Rainforest

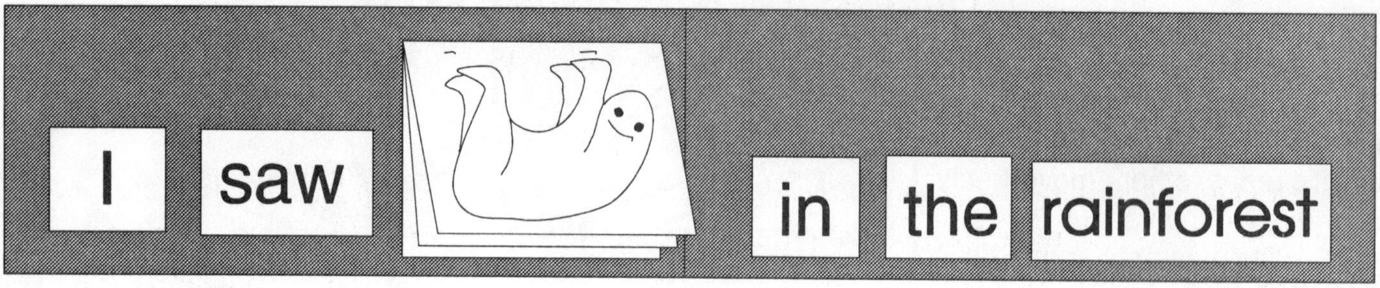

Use the animals of the rainforest as the subject of child-created books. After students have discussed what animals can be found in the rainforest, they can create their own flipbooks to share with their families.

Materials:

- a 9" x 12" (22.8 x 30.5 cm) sheet of green construction paper
- a copy of the word cards shown below
- several white 4" x 5" (10 x 13 cm) construction paper rectangles

Steps to follow:

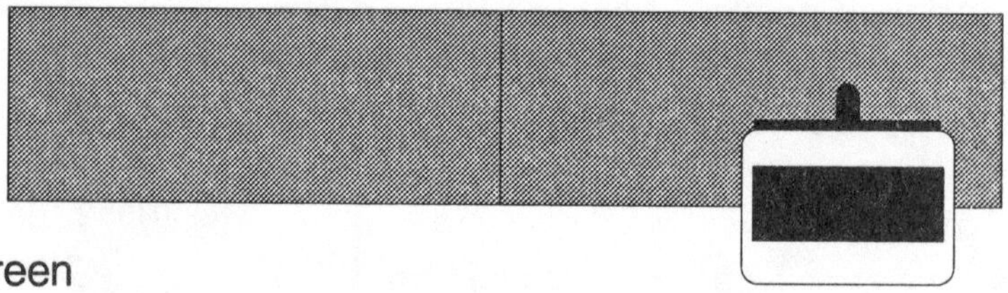

1. Cut the green paper in half the long way. Glue the pieces together.
2. Cut the word cards apart and glue to the green paper as shown.
3. Staple the white rectangles to the green paper to create the flipbook.
4. Draw a picture of a different animal found in the rainforest on each flip page.

I

saw

in

the

rainforest.

Note: Display books with pictures of the animal being studied for your children to enjoy.

Animals of the Rainforest

Teacher Information

Insects (pages 15-16)

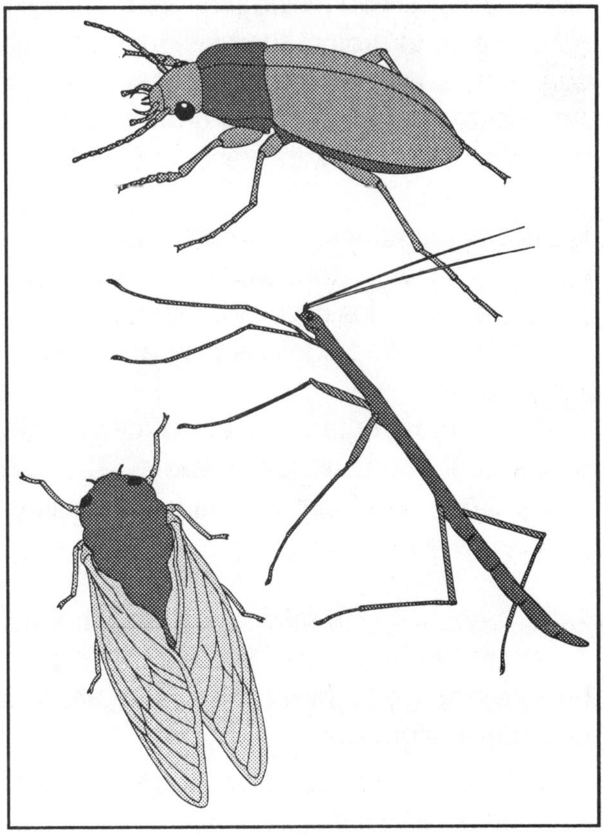

Over half of the world's insects live in the rainforests. There are more insects in the forest than any other type of animal. Many species have not yet been discovered. The rainforest's warm, moist climate allows some of these insects to grow to huge sizes.

Although we consider most insects pests, they are an important part of the food chain. Bats, birds, spiders, frogs and snakes all eat insects. The insects also help by eating rotted plants, leaves, wood and other insects.

Insects have six legs. They have antennae on their heads. They use the antennae to hear and to find food. Some insects can smell scents as far as a mile away. Many of these insects use camouflage to hide among the jungle plants. Some look like leaves, thorns, or twigs.

Ask your students to name as many insects as they can in one minute.

Ants (pages 17-23)

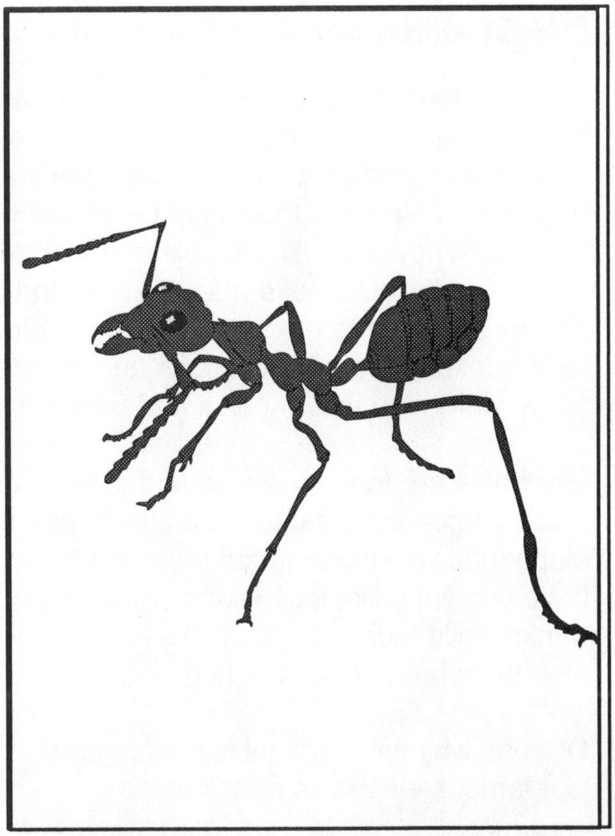

Ants are one of the many kinds of insects found in the rainforest. There are many different kinds of ants there. Two interesting types are the leaf-cutter ant and the army (driver) ant.

The leaf-cutter ant lives on the forest floor. It travels a long way to carry pieces of green leaves back to its colony. The ant "plants" the leaves in one of the chambers in the colony to grow a kind of mold. They eat this for food.

The army (driver) ant is like a hunter. These ants will eat and destroy anything in their path. An army ant eats small mammals, insects, even rarely a human. The sun is an enemy to these ants. They stay out of the sun by working at night.

Boa Constrictors (pages 24-29)

Boa constrictors are a kind of snake. Like all snakes they have no legs, but they can still get around quickly using their strong muscles. They have their hearts, lungs, etc., spread inside their long bodies. They have hard scales to protect their insides from injury. Boa constrictors are the second-largest snake in the Americas. They live on the ground, but they do climb trees and hang on with prehensile tails.

Boas are found mostly in New World forests. They live on the ground, in trees and in or near water. Boa babies develop inside their mother's body. They hatch out of thin-shelled eggs as they are born.

Boas are meat eaters. They squeeze their prey to suffocate it, then swallow it whole. Their body color and pattern help them to hide while waiting for their prey.

Other boas living in rainforests are emerald tree boas. They are bright green. Emerald tree boas live in trees, but are also good swimmers. They are smaller than boa constrictors.

Elephants (pages 30-35)

Elephants are the largest land mammal living today. They are strong and intelligent. They travel in herds, looking after one another, especially the young. Their huge ears help keep them cool by allowing heat to escape. They use tusks to split bark and to dig up roots. Their trunks have many nerves and muscles. Trunks are used to touch and to smell. Elephants use their trunks to grab leaves, fruits and shoots and to spray water into their mouths and over their bodies.

Elephants are found in Africa and in India (a part of Asia). African elephants are a little bigger than Indian elephants, with much larger ears and tusks. They have two fingerlike extensions at the end of their trunks while Indian elephants have only one. Indian elephants have more of a humped back.

Discuss why the elephant is endangered.
List famous elephants from literature.

Frogs (pages 36-39)

Frogs are amphibians. An amphibian is an animal that lives in the water and on land. (Have children see if they can name any animals that do this.) One type of amphibian is the frog. Most frogs begin their lives in water. When fully grown, frogs will live part of the time on land.

Frogs differ in the various rainforests around the world. They come in many different sizes. They come in different colors. The Poison Arrow Frog is only 1/2 inch (1.3 cm) long, while the Goliath Frog is 32 inches (43.5 cm) long and can weigh up to seven pounds (3.15 kilograms). Some are green or greenish brown to blend in with the foliage, but others are very bright colors.

Gorillas (pages 40-43)

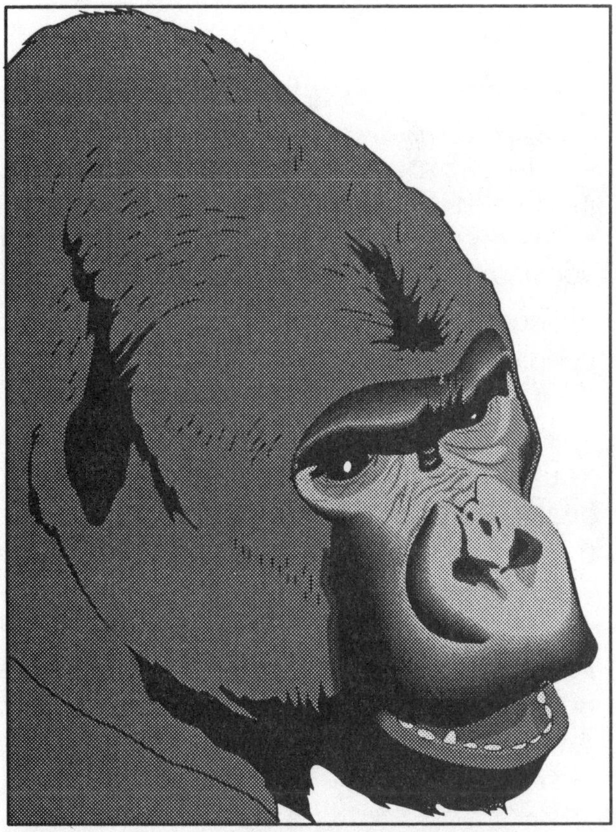

Gorillas live in groups of five to thirty. These groups are called troops. They are strong, gentle animals. Gorillas live in the dense African jungles with a lot of different plants. They eat huge amounts of fruits and vegetation every day.

A gorilla walks by placing the knuckles of its hands and soles of its feet on the ground. (Have children try to walk like a gorilla.) The habitat of the gorilla is being destroyed. Many of the trees the gorilla lives in are being cut down so that coffee and other foods can be grown and sold. If man continues to cut down the trees, the gorilla will have no place to live or food to eat.

Sloths (pages 44-46)

Sloths are slow-moving mammals living in the jungles of Central and South America. They hang from branches because this uses less energy than balancing on them. Sloths have curved, sharp claws that hook over branches. Sloths eat all kinds of leaves (any close at hand) and hang quietly while bacteria in their stomachs help to digest the leaves. Since they move so slowly, sloths cannot escape from danger. So they try to blend into their surroundings. Their coarse hair is filled with algae. This gives a greenish tint to their fur and helps camouflage them. They are hunted by eagles. The eagles watch for movement as the sloths go out into sunny spots to warm up. The slow sloth cannot escape, so it is carried off by the eagle.

Birds (pages 47-49)

Rainforests are full of fruit, flowers and insects. All the things birds like to eat. The rainforests of the world are filled with birds of all sizes, shapes and colors. Some live near the dark jungle floor, some live in the branches of short trees, others live in the tall trees and some fly up into the canopy.

These birds are each adapted to their own type of life. You can tell a lot about what a bird eats by looking at its beak. Small brightly colored hummingbirds, big-beaked toucans, rare eagles all add their calls to this rich environment.

In this unit, we will learn about toucans. They are large, brightly colored birds found in the forests of South America.

Insects

An insect has six legs.

An insect has two antennae.

Insects hear with their antennae.

They smell food with their antennae.

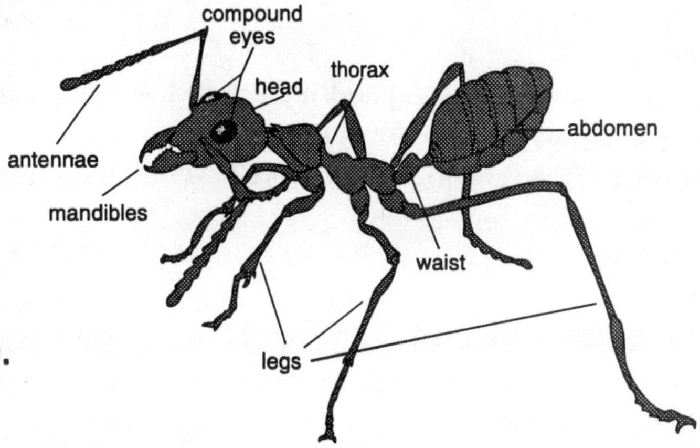

There are many different insects in the rainforest.
Circle the insects.

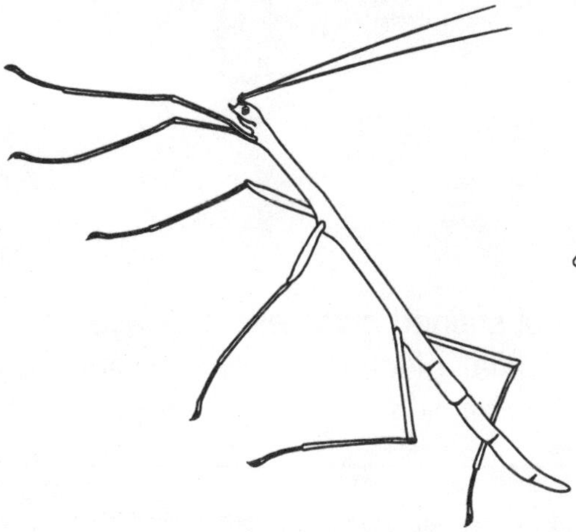
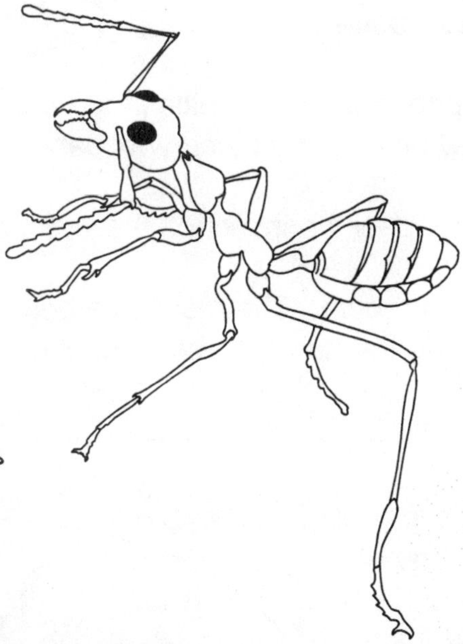

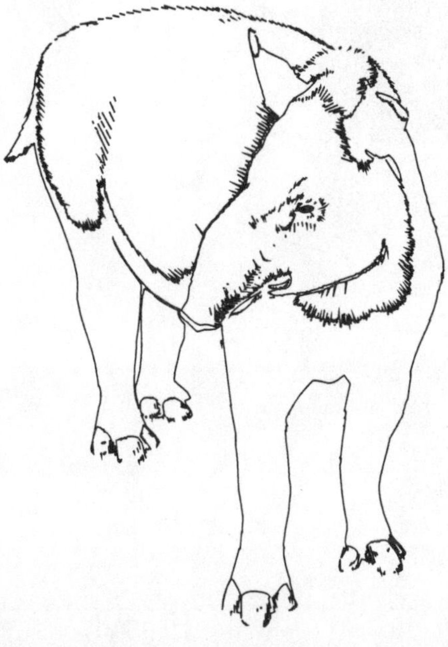
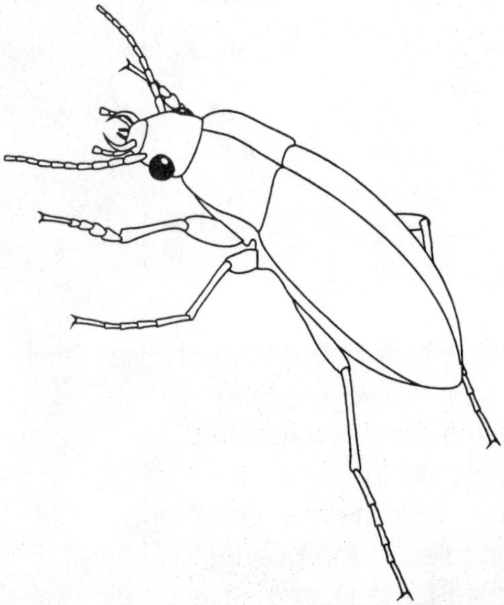
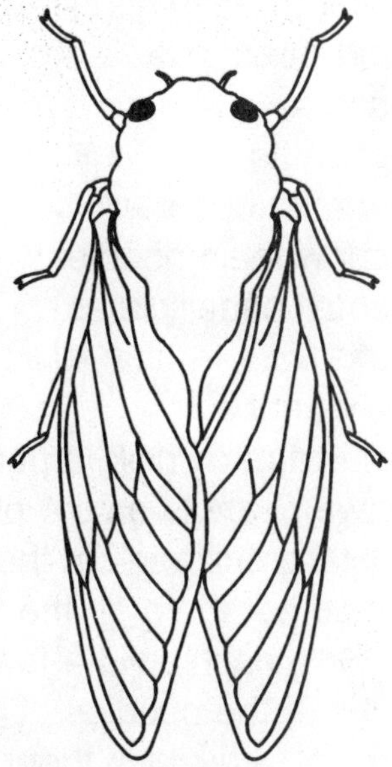

Note: There is a colored glue sold by Elmer's that can be used for this activity.

Insect Window Stickers

Have your students imagine they are in the rainforest and have just discovered a new insect.
What does this new insect look like? What is its name?

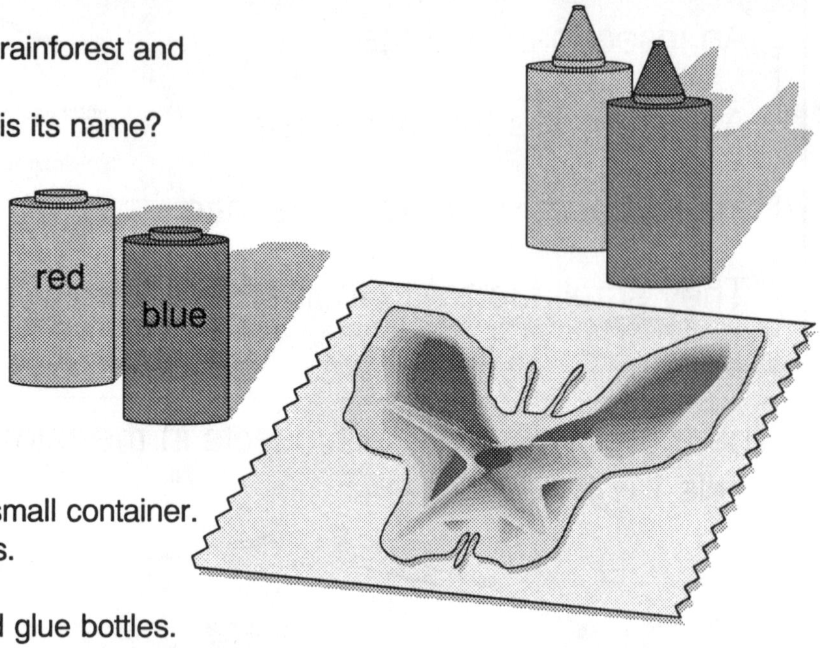

Materials:
- glue
- powder tempera paint
- wax paper
- squeeze bottles
- container and spoon for mixing

Procedures:
1. Mix the tempera paint with the glue in a small container. Pour the colored glue into squeeze bottles.

2. Give each child a piece of wax paper and glue bottles. They use the glue bottles to draw an insect on their wax paper.

3. Let the glue insects dry. Carefully peel the insect off the wax paper.

4. Tape the insects to a window in the room. The result is a beautiful stained glass effect. Have children print (or have teacher print) the name of their insect on a small piece of paper and tape it by their insect.

Edible Bugs

Have your students make bugs they can eat for snacks.

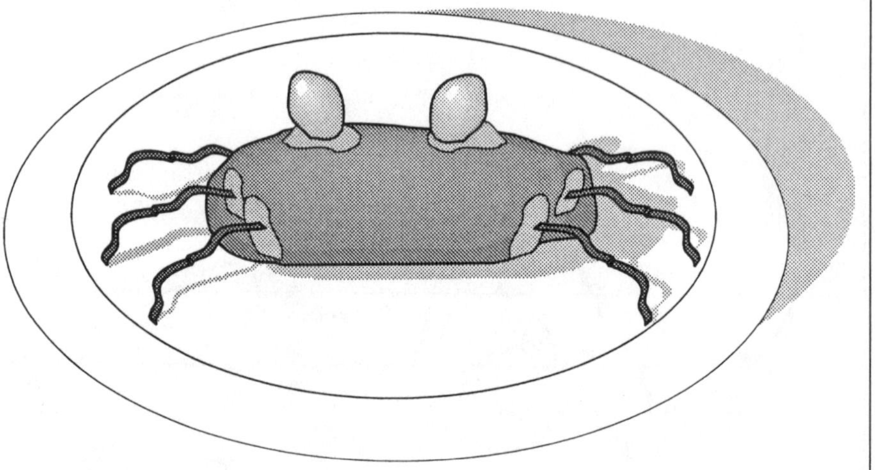

Materials:
- dates
- peanuts
- peanut butter
- chow mein noodles
- small paper plates

Procedure:
1. Give each child a paper plate. Place one date and two peanuts on the plate.
2. Have children dip the peanuts in the peanut butter and put them on the top of the date for eyes.
3. Give each child a few noodles. Ask them to count out six of the noodles. Dip the noodles in the peanut butter and stick them in the date for legs.

Enjoy!

Ants

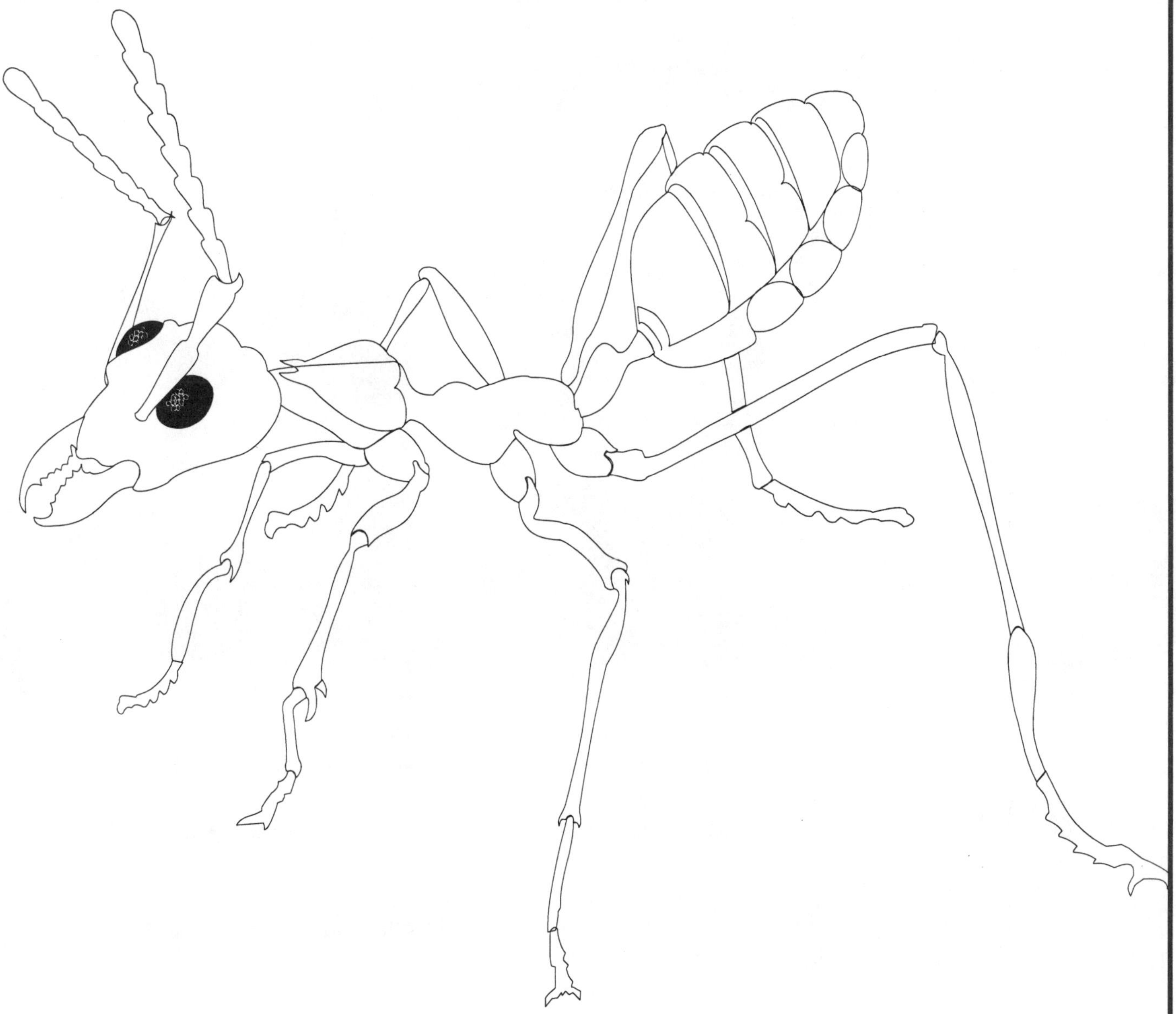

Ants are a kind of insect.
There are many different kinds of ants in the rainforest.
This is a **leaf-cutter ant**. Color it.

Note: Read ***Ant Cities*** by Arthur Dorros to your students.

Ant Hill
Bulletin Board

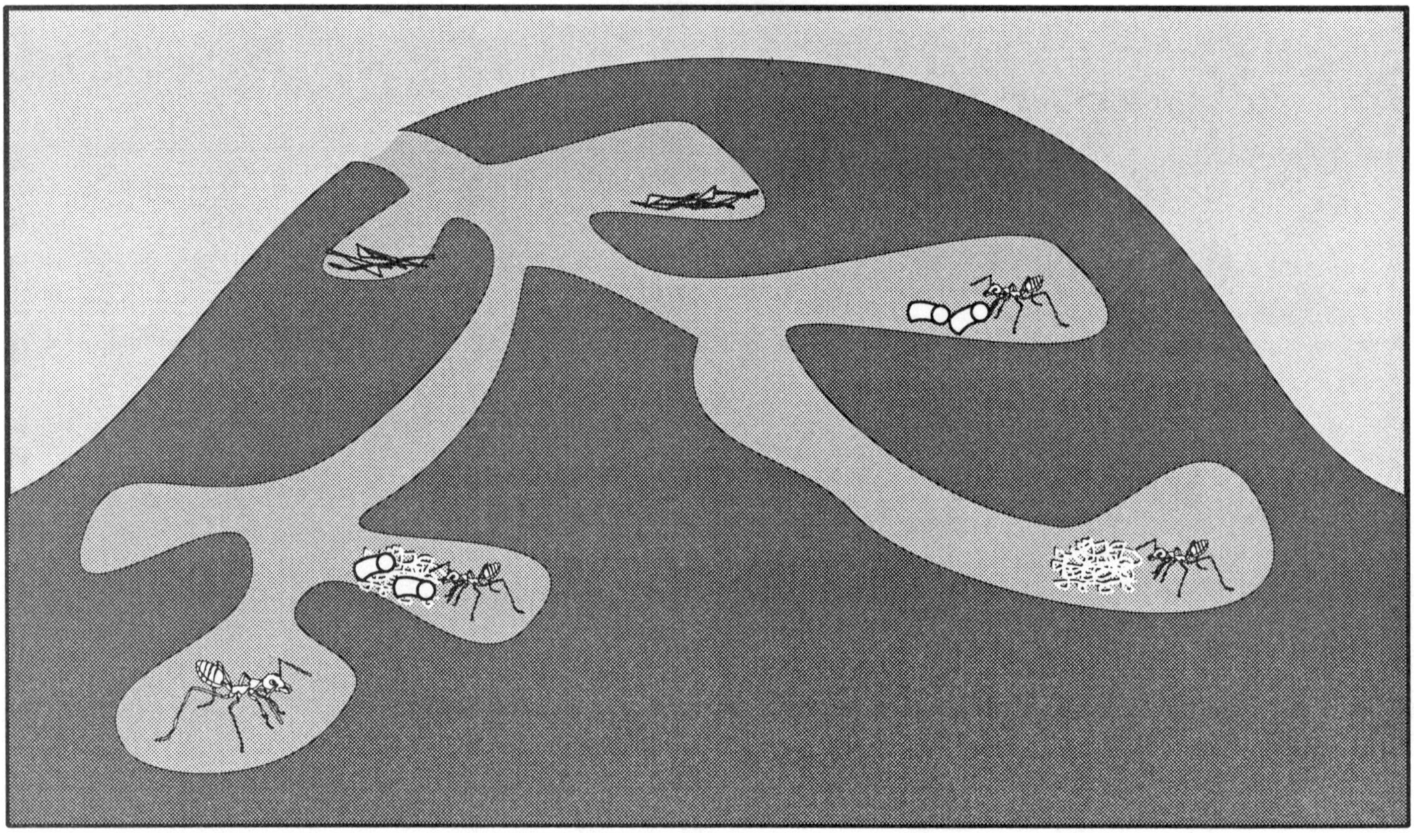

Draw a large ant hill on brown butcher paper. Divide it into chambers. Draw tunnels to connect the chambers. Mount the ant hill on a bulletin board being sure it is low enough for your students to reach.

Make copies of the ant patterns on page 23. Color and cut out the patterns and place the ants in the correct chambers of the ant hill.

Discuss with your students the job each ant has in the colony. Divide your students into four groups. They are going to be the ants for this colony.

Group 1 - **Workers**
They tear small pieces of green paper to represent leaves.
Have them glue these "leaves" in the correct chamber.

Group 2 -**Queen Ant and Eggs**
The children in this group glue styrofoam balls representing eggs in the nursery chamber.
Enlarge one ant pattern to represent the queen.

Group 3 - **Gardeners**
Have children make "mushrooms" from cotton balls. They stretch them out and glue them in the correct chamber.

Group 4 - **Nursery Workers and Ant Larva**
Have children glue macaroni pieces in the correct chamber to represent the ant "larva."

Life in an Ant Hill

Color the pictures.

Cut out the wheel and ant hill.

Put the pieces together with a paper fastener.

Turn the wheel and tell the life story of an ant.

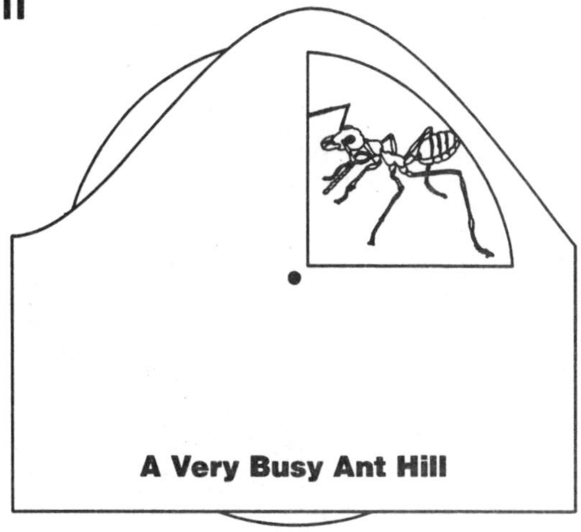

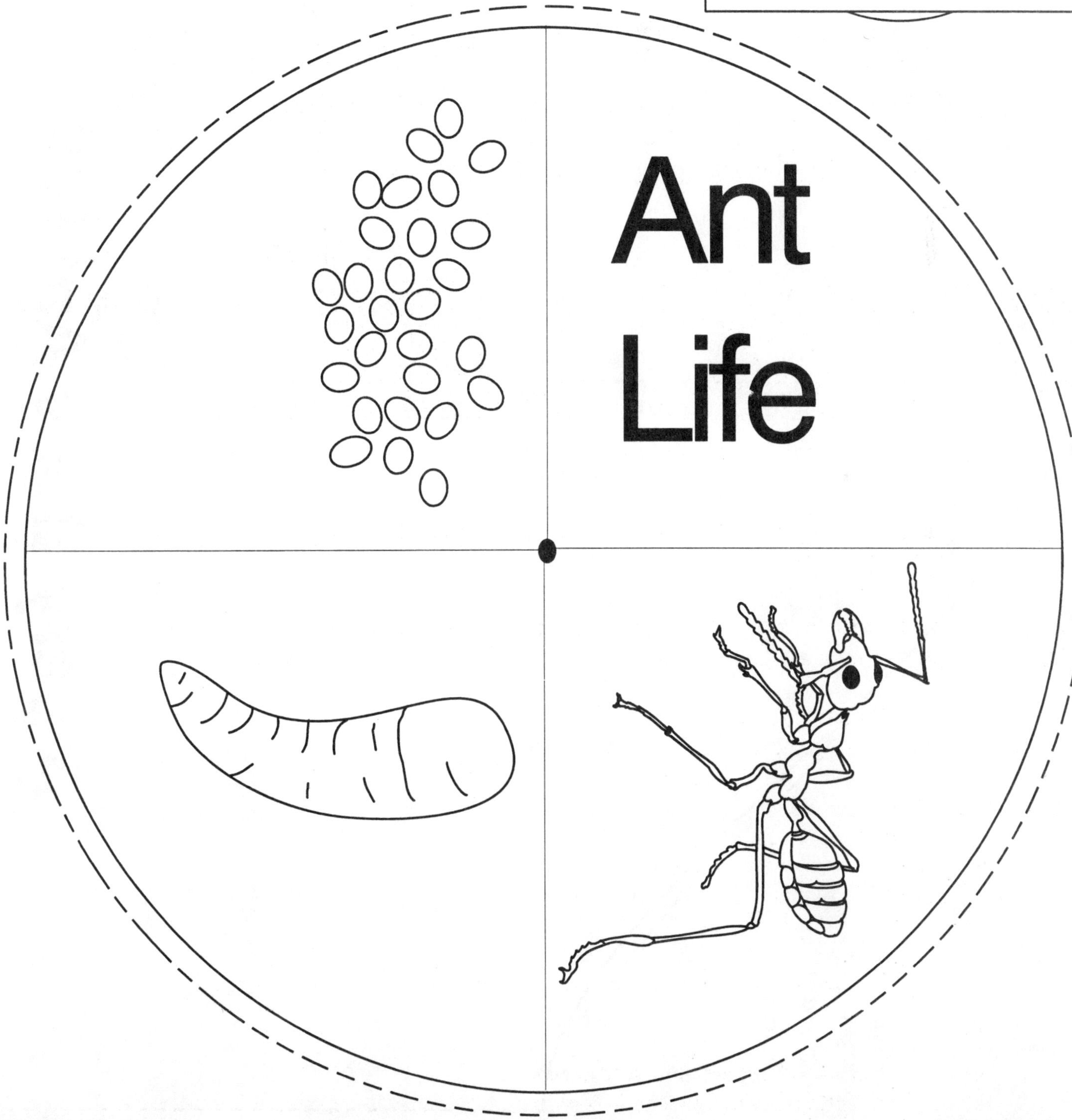

Note: Reproduce the patterns on this and the following page for each child. Teacher or another adult will need to make the "window" cut for younger children.

Ant Hill Pattern

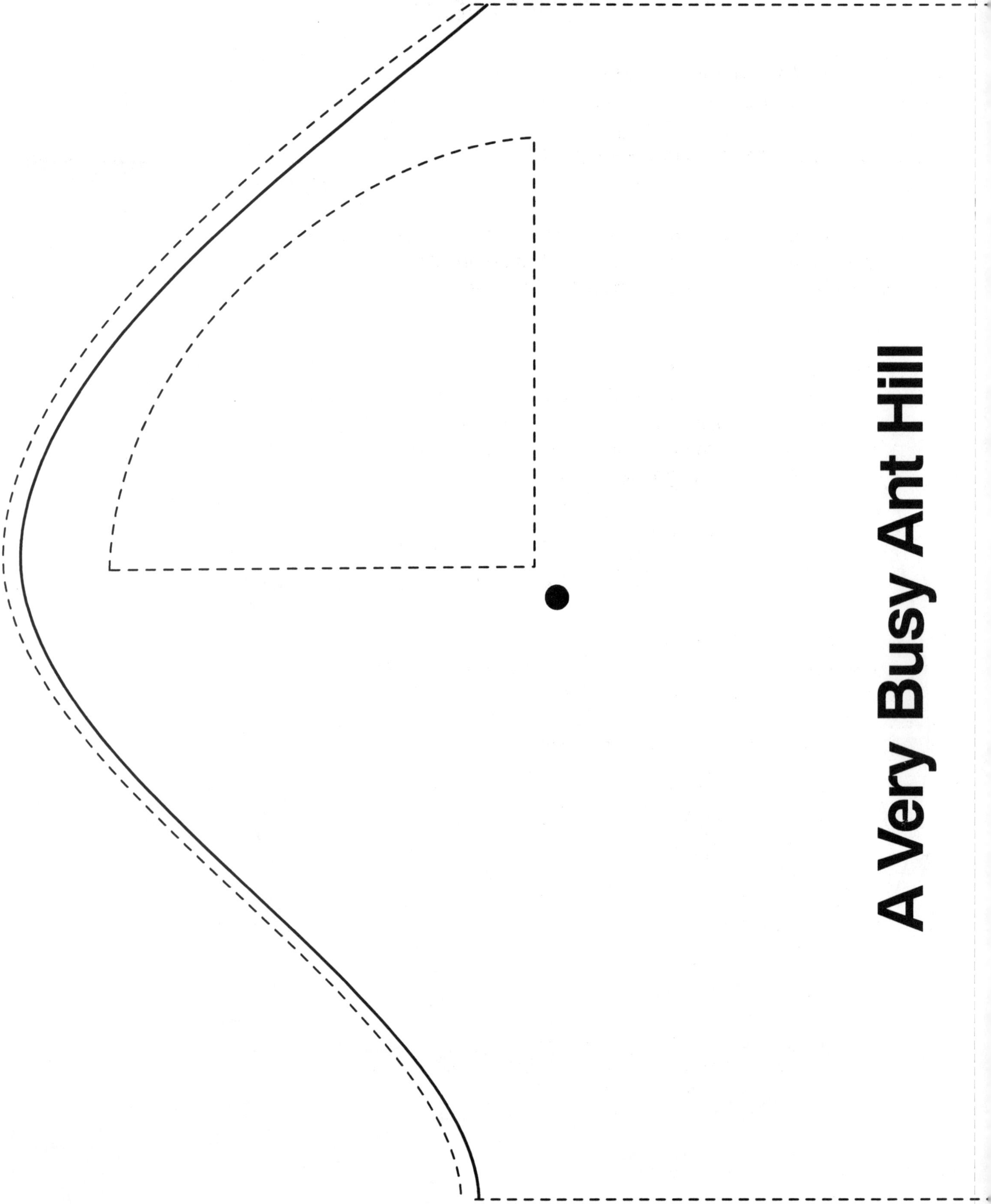

Note: Use your flannel board to practice math skills. If you do not have a flannel board, make the pieces from paper and pin them to a bulletin board.

Ant Math

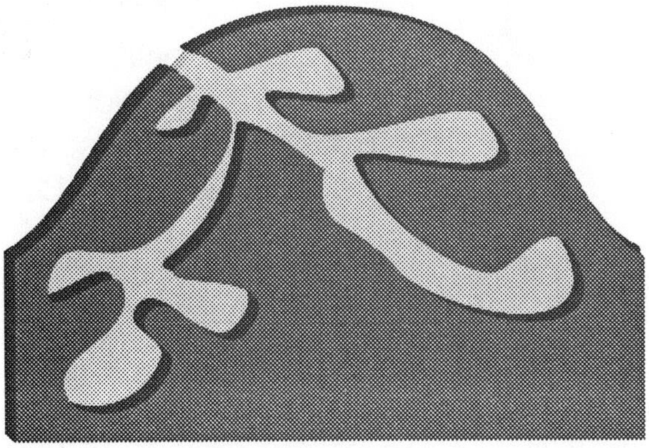

Cut an ant hill from brown felt. Cut ant tunnels from beige felt and lay over the brown felt. Reproduce several of the ant patterns on this page. Glue a piece of Pellon or Velcro to the back of the ant pieces.

More or Less:

Place the ant hill on your flannel board. Place one ant outside of the ant hill. Place two ants inside the hill. Ask "Are there more ants in the hill or outside of the hill?" "Who would like to change the ants so there will be more ants outside than inside?" Continue this procedure several times.

Ordinal Numbers/Geometric Shapes:

Make a set of geometric shapes from different colors of felt. Use the pieces with these math activities. Place your geometric shapes in a row. Put one ant on each geometric shape. Ask "What shape is the third ant standing on?" "Is the fifth ant standing on a square?" "Which ant is standing on the last shape?" Have children rearrange the pieces on the flannel board, then repeat your questions.

Readiness for Computation:

Place the ant hill on the flannel board. Select a child to place one or more ants on the hill. Ask "How many ants do you see on the ant hill?" "If I put one more ant on the hill, how many will you see?" "If I take away three ants, how many will be left?" Continue adding and subtracting ants, using only amounts that are appropriate for your students.

Make an Ant Book

Ants are not just black. They can also be red, yellow, blue...even green! To reinforce color and color word recognition, make an Ant Color Book in one of these formats. You can use the same directions to create an Ant Counting Book.

Big Book:

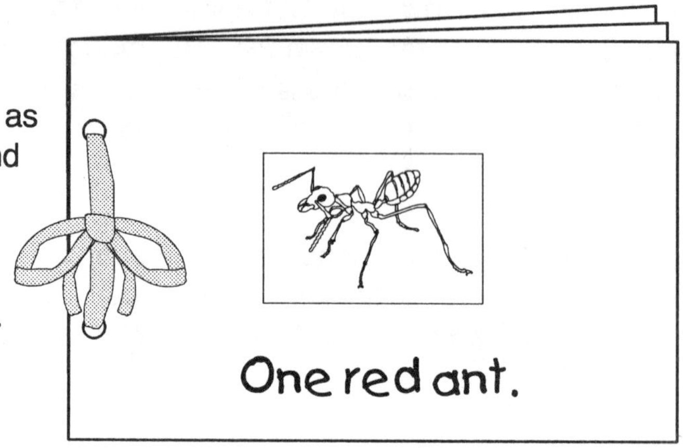

Enlarge the patterns on the following page to create as many ants as you need for your book. Color, cut and paste the pictures to 12" X 18" (30.5 x 45.7 cm) sheets of construction paper or tagboard. Write the words for your story using marking pen. Staple the pages into a cover. Here is one possible story form.

One red ant.
One blue ant.
One yellow ant.
One green ant.
One black ant.
One anteater.
Run, ants, run!

Wee Ant Color Book:

Reproduce the same pictures, but do not enlarge them. Have your students color, cut and paste 4 1/2" x 6" (11.3 x 15 cm) sheets of paper. Have them write the words at the bottom of the pages. If your students are not ready to write, give them pages already containing the words. Staple the pages together in a cover of construction paper. Send the book home for the child to share with his/her parents.

Ant Counting Book:

Follow the same steps to create a Big Counting Book or a Wee Counting Book. This time page one will have one ant, page two will have two ants, etc., as high as you wish to go. Here is a sample book you might create. You may want students to darw their own ants.

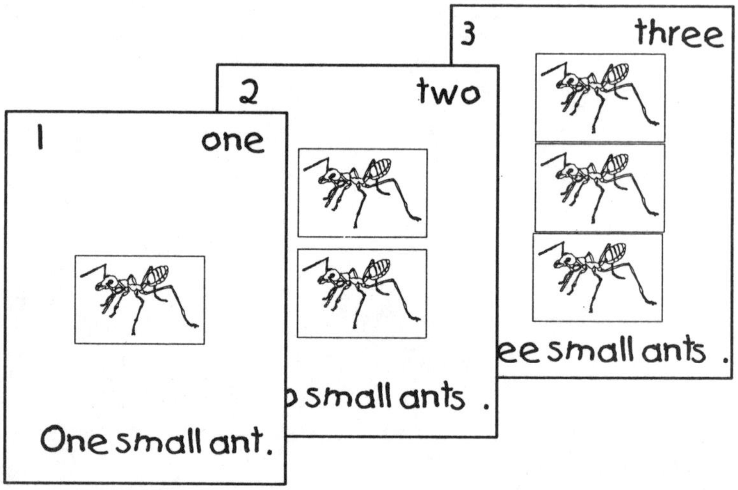

One small ant.
Two small ants.
Three small ants.
Four small ants.
Five small ants.
One hungry anteater.
Run, ants, run!

Patterns

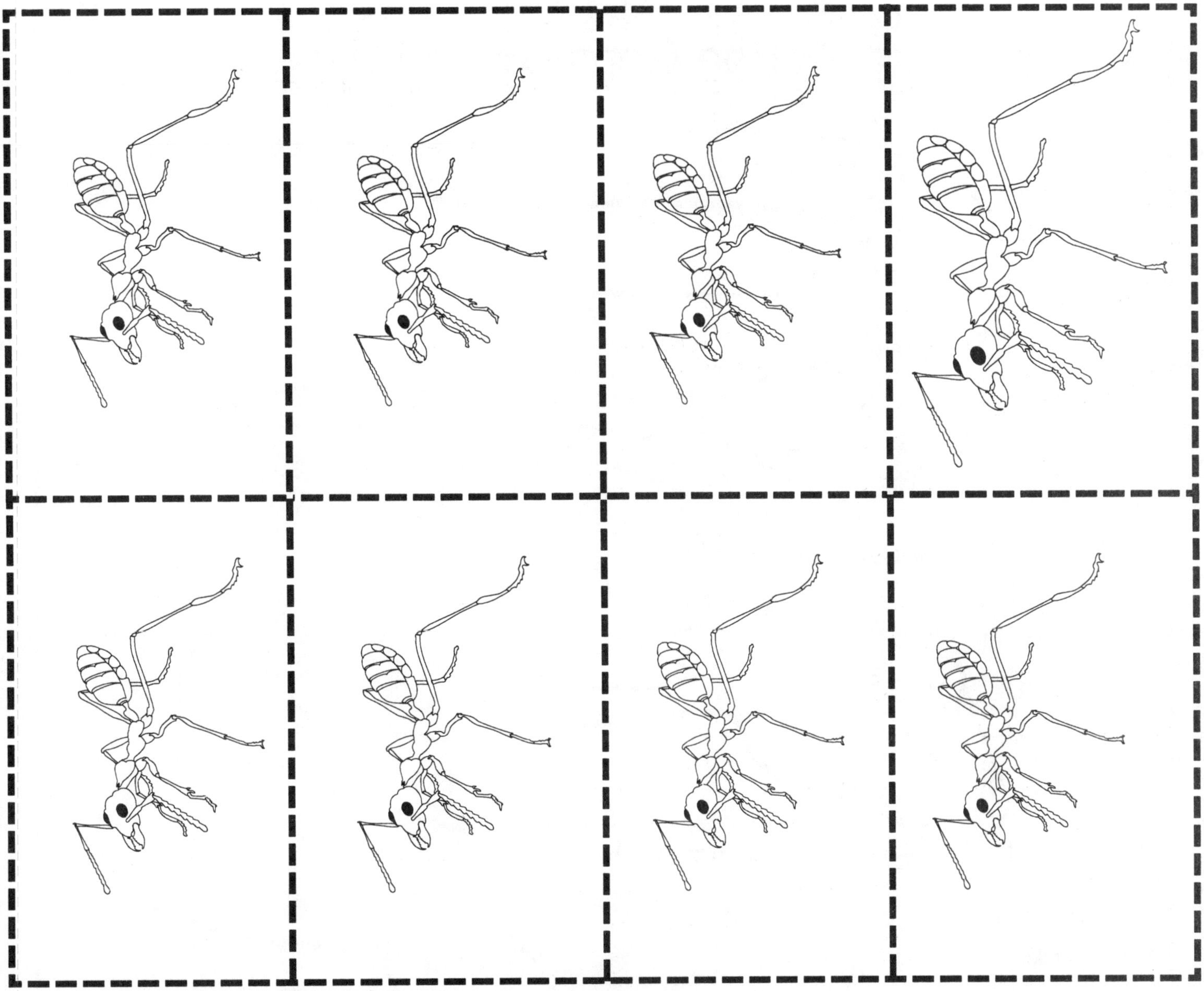

Boa Constrictors

Boa constrictors are large snakes.
They live on the ground.
Emerald boas are smaller than boa constrictors.
They live in trees.
Both snakes squeeze their prey and swallow it whole.

Color the boa constrictor brown.
Color the emerald boa green.

Boa Reading and Language Activities

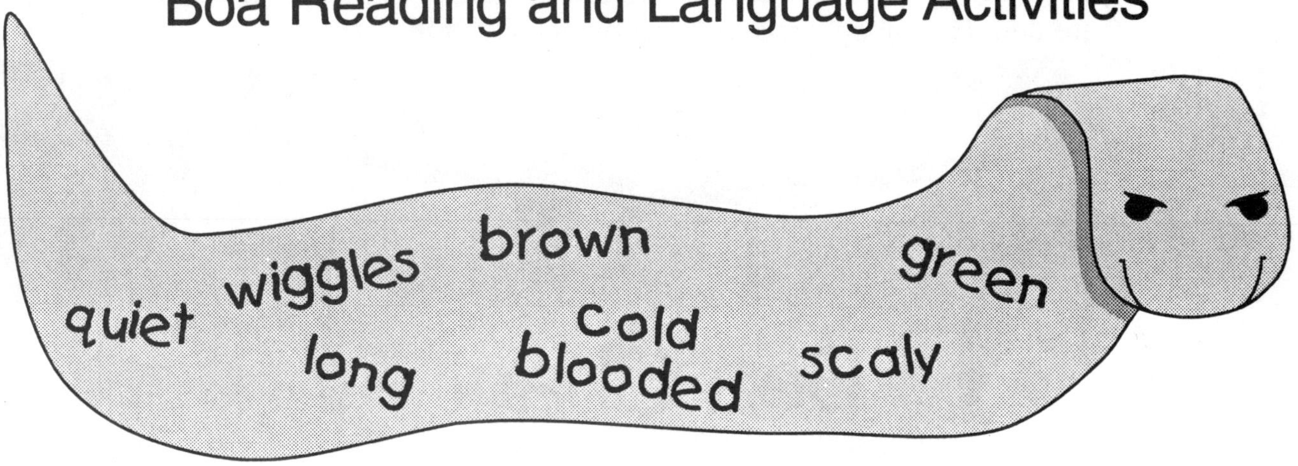

• **Descriptive Language -** Read ***The Day Jimmy's Boa Ate the Wash*** by Trinka Hakes Nobel or another snake book to your children. Ask students to name words that describe a boa. Write these words on a large laminated boa constrictor. Keep this list of words up for children who are ready to read/write to use as a word list.

• **Spell Boa -** Pass out sets of letter cards that spell the word "boa." Ask children to tell you the sound that boa begins with. Have them find that card and place it in front of them. Ask them to tell you the second sound in boa. Have them locate the card that shows that letter and place it after the first card. Ask them to then place the final card in its correct place. Ask "How do you spell boa?" and have them touch each letter as they say it.

• **"Boa Constrictor Song" -** Read this poem from ***Where the Sidewalk Ends*** by Shel Silverstein to your children. Have them repeat it after you as they act it out.

• **Boa Letters -** Give each child a hunk of clay. Have them roll the clay into the shape of a snake. Hold up a card showing a letter (or write it on the chalkboard) and have children form the letter with their clay snake.

• **Boa Bracelet -** Reinforce the letter "B" and its sound by making boa bracelets. Give each child a copy of the pattern shown below. They color and cut out their boa. Then they tape the tail to the mouth around their wrists.

Boa Chant - Ask your children to find all the "B's" and count them. Have them find the word "Boa" and count how many there are. Have them recite and act out the chant.

Boa Chant

Boa, Boa, turn around.

Boa, Boa, touch the ground.

Boa, Boa, slither up the tree.

Boa, Boa, stay away from me.

Boa, Boa, I don't want to be,

Boa, Boa, in your tum-my!

Science

Discuss the boa's diet. The boa crushes small animals and swallows them whole. Its diet consists of mice, pigs, otters, pacas and other small mammals and reptiles.

The Expandable Emerald Boa

Make a boa with a full tummy following these directions.

1. Paste two 6" X 18" (15 x 45.7 cm) pieces of green construction paper together. Fold as shown below.

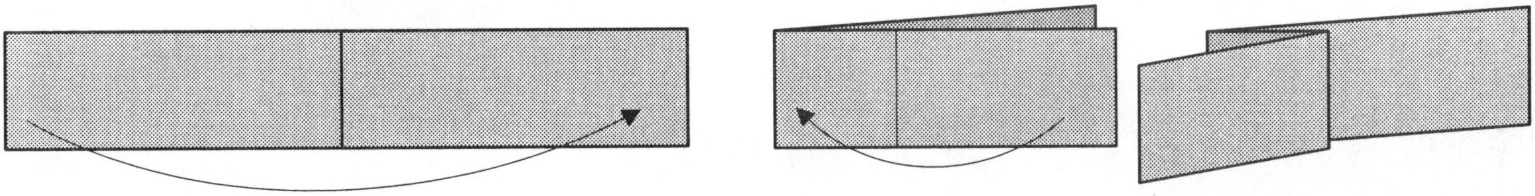

2. Round off the corners of one end and cut the other end to a point. Add two eyes for the boa's head.

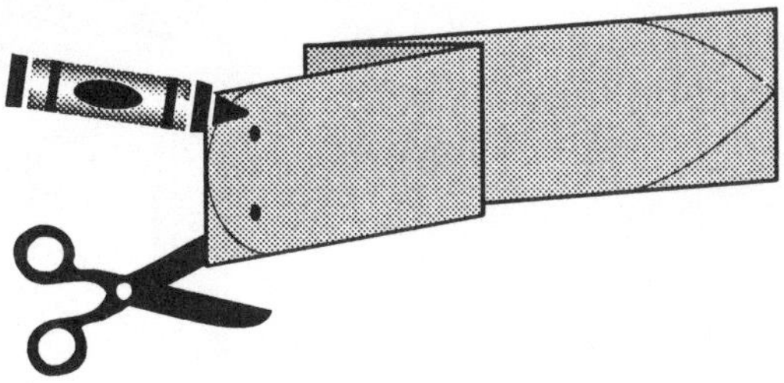

3. Draw what the boa ate in the middle space.

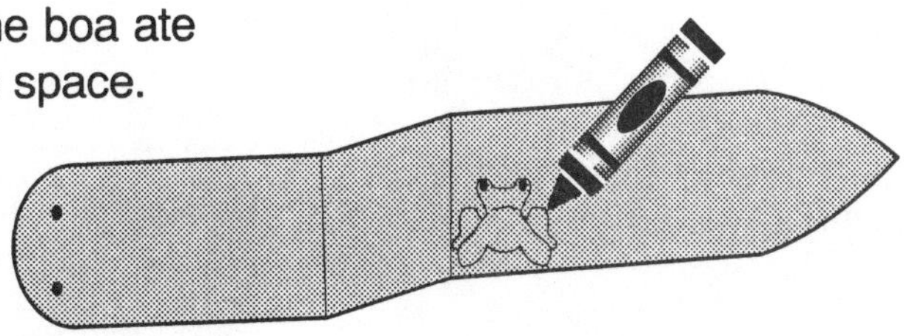

"My Boa's Bigger"

Have children sing this song to the tune of "My Dog's Bigger than Your Dog." Select a child to show what his/her boa ate and use this "food" as the last word of the song. Repeat several times using a different child's boa each time.

My boa's bigger than your boa.

My boa's bigger than yours.

My boa's bigger than your boa

'Cause he eats lots of _______

Note: If your students are ready to begin standard measurement, reproduce the boa ruler on the following page for your students. Explore measuring in inches, centimeters or both.

Boa Math

Non-Standard Measurement:

1. Teach measurement with boa "rulers." Have each child draw and color a boa. The boas can be any length or color. Cut the boas out and show how to measure objects such as a table, desk or door using the boa as a ruler. Ask questions such as "How many boas tall is this desk?" "How many boas wide is this door?"

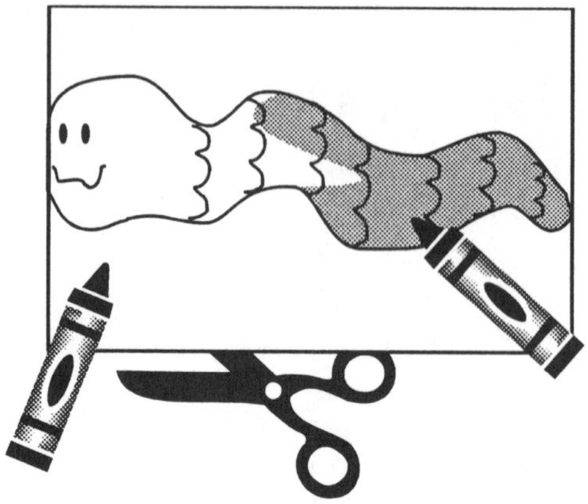

2. Select one item in the room. Choose five children to measure it with their boas. Record the number of boas on the chalkboard. Discuss why children have different answers to the same measurement question. (Their snakes are different sizes.)

3. Divide children into pairs to measure their heights in boas. Help them write down their answers.

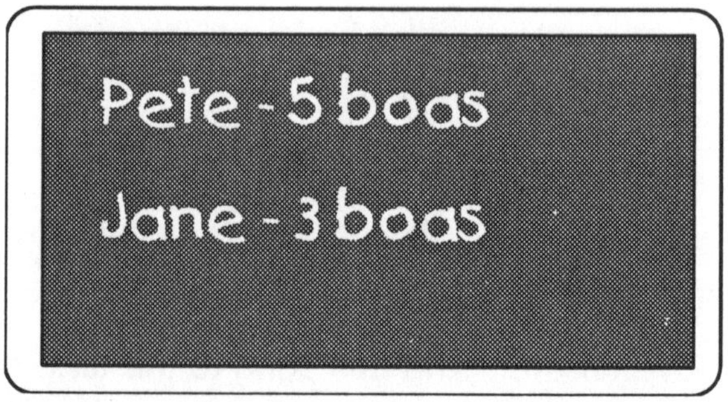

Comparisons:

Help your children develop the language of comparisons using their boas. Select several of the boas made by the children. Place them on a bulletin board or chalktray so everyone can see them. Ask questions requiring comparisons.

Which boa is the longest?

Which boa is the fattest?

Can you choose a boa that is larger than this one?

Who can put the boas in order from the longest to the shortest?

Boa Constrictor Ruler

Cut out the ruler pieces. Paste or tape them together.

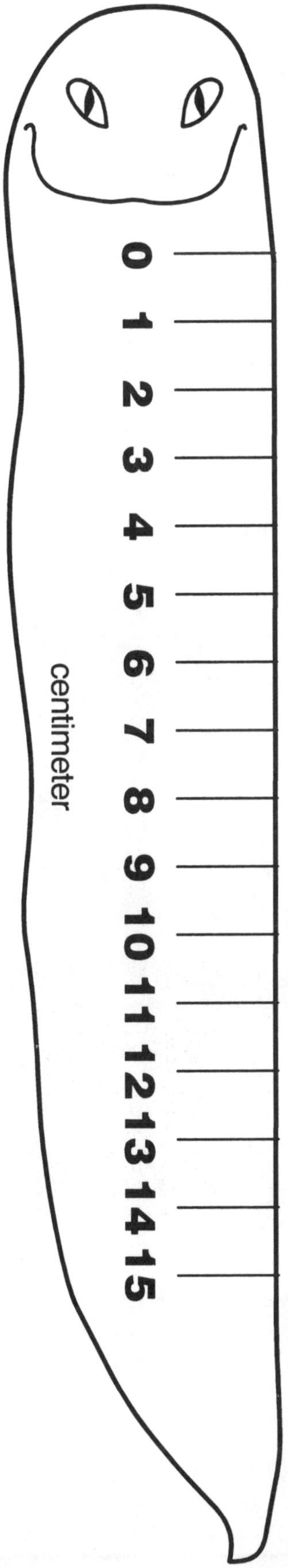

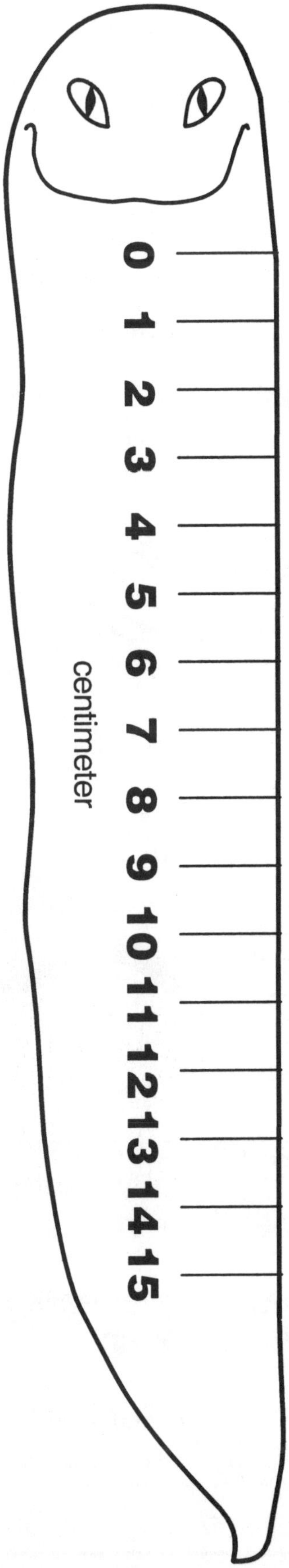

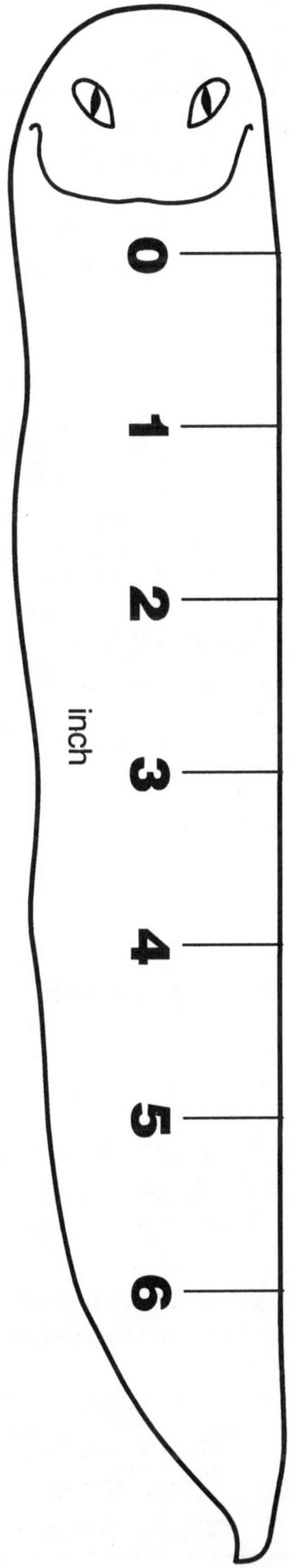

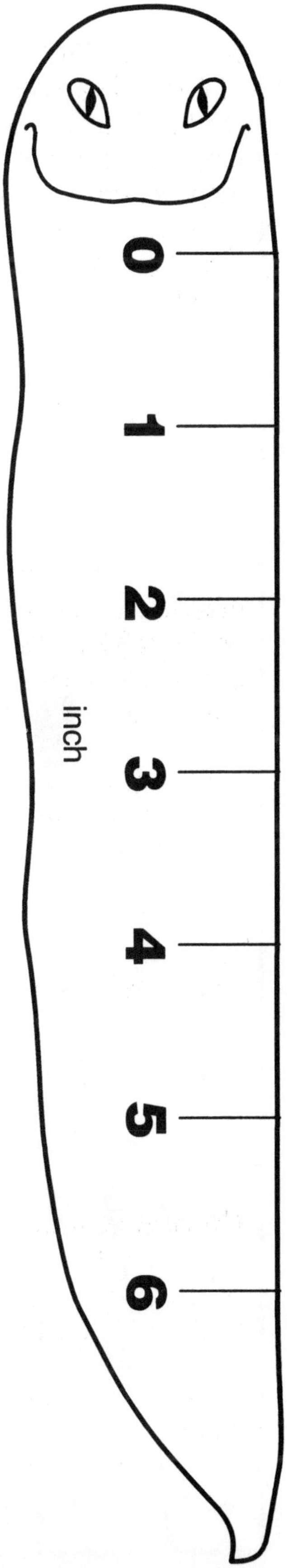

Elephants

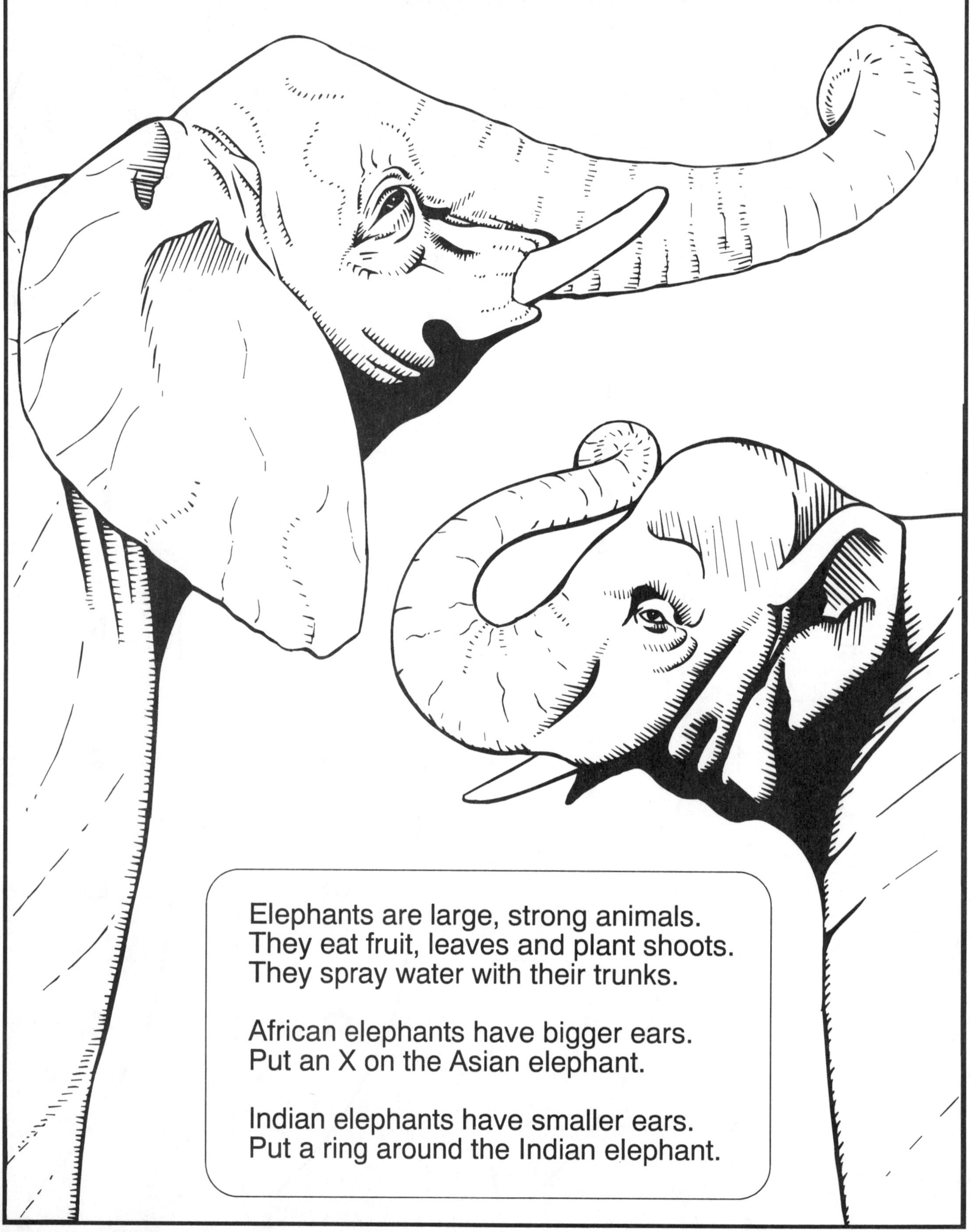

Elephants are large, strong animals.
They eat fruit, leaves and plant shoots.
They spray water with their trunks.

African elephants have bigger ears.
Put an X on the Asian elephant.

Indian elephants have smaller ears.
Put a ring around the Indian elephant.

Fungle in the Jungle

The elephant moved very slowly.
His trunk was dragging the ground.
He was feeling kind of lonely,
But then his friends came around.

And they had...
FUNGLE,
FUNGLE,
FUNGLE
In the jungle.
The elephants go fungle
In the jungle.
FUNGLE,
FUNGLE,
FUNGLE,
The elephants go fungle
In the jungle.

from *Fungle in the Jungle*
by Debbie de Pauw

Elephant Headband

Follow the directions below to make elephant headbands.
Have children wear their headbands as they chant *"Fungle in the Jungle"* and stomp around the room.

Materials for each student:

- 2 sheets of 12" x 18" (30.5 x 45.7 cm) gray construction paper
- scissors, crayons and a stapler

Steps to follow:

1. Precut the construction paper according to this format:

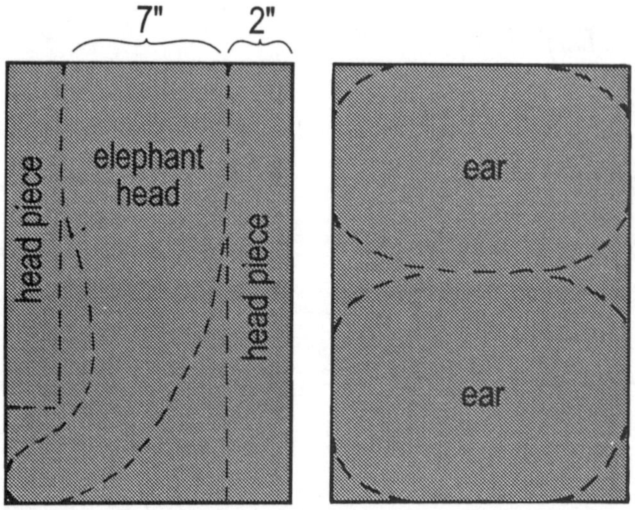

2. Students may color their elephant parts.
3. Fold the head piece down and cut the eye holes.
4. Staple the headband to fit the student's head.
5. Staple on the elephant head and trunk piece to the headband while the student is wearing the band.
6. Now staple on the two ears.

Elephant Math

Counting 1 - 10:

Teach this refrain...

> Walking through the jungle,
> Doing the "Fungle,"
> How many times did the elephant stomp?

Select a child to be the elephant. Have this child walk around as his/her classmates chant the refrain. When they are through the "elephant child" stomps out any number from one to ten. The other children count the number of stomps and either say that number or hold up a card showing the number.

Or place number cards 1-10 in a box in the center of a ring of children. Each child draws a number. The child says his/her number and everyone else pounds out that number of "stomps."

Computation:

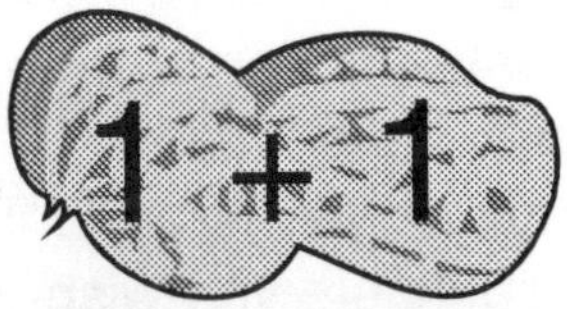

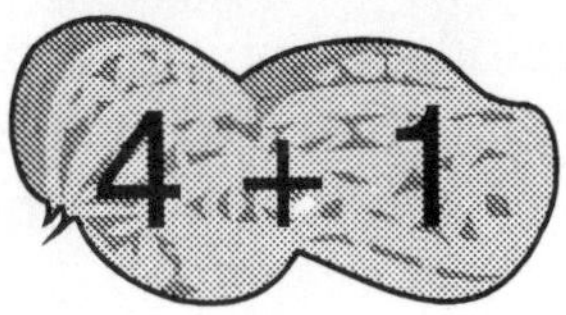

Reproduce the peanuts using the patterns on the bottom of this page. Write an addition problem on each peanut. Children select a "problem peanut" and use real peanuts to solve the problem. You can make the problem cards self-correcting by writing the answer on the back of the card, covering it with a flap which the child can lift to check his/her answer.

Other Peanut Math Activities:

1. Draw a number card and count out that many peanuts. You may want older children to write the number and draw the number of peanuts shown.

2. Glue sets of peanuts to cards. Make cards with the symbols for *more, less, equal to*. Children lay out peanuts and symbols to show relationships.

3. Have children make numbers by gluing peanuts into the number shape.

Eat peanuts just for fun!

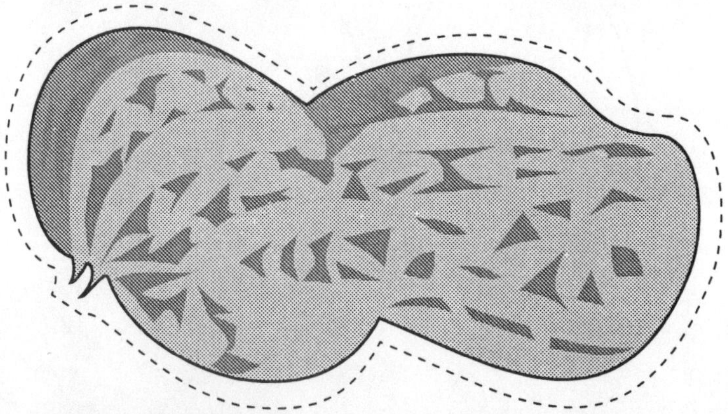

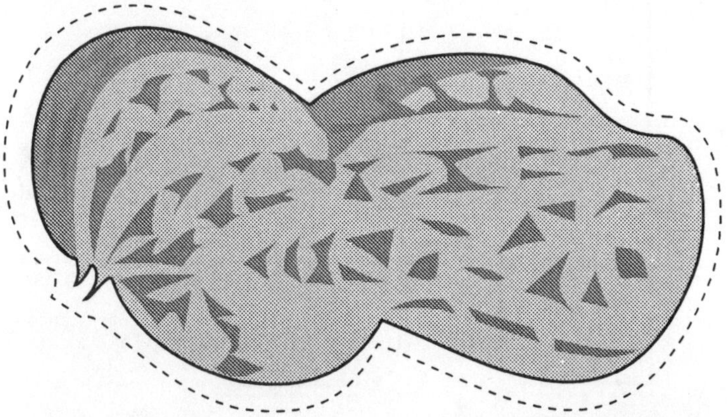

Elephant Language Activities

Elephant Letter Hunt:
Print the letters that spell "elephant" on index cards. Display these letters. Have children identify each letter as you name it. Next, have children close their eyes as you remove a letter. See if they can name the missing letter. Repeat this several times with different letters. Ask for volunteers to find the first letter, second letter, etc. Finally, scramble the letters and see if by working together the children can put the letters into their correct order. (You may want to mix up only two or three letters to begin with.)

Capital/Lower Case Letter Identification:
Use the patterns on this page for matching capital and lower case letters. Make copies of as many of the patterns as you need to fill in the capital letters and lower case letters you wish your children to practice, then reproduce copies for the group or class. Children draw lines to make correct matches. The form may be used over and over by changing what is written on the leaves.

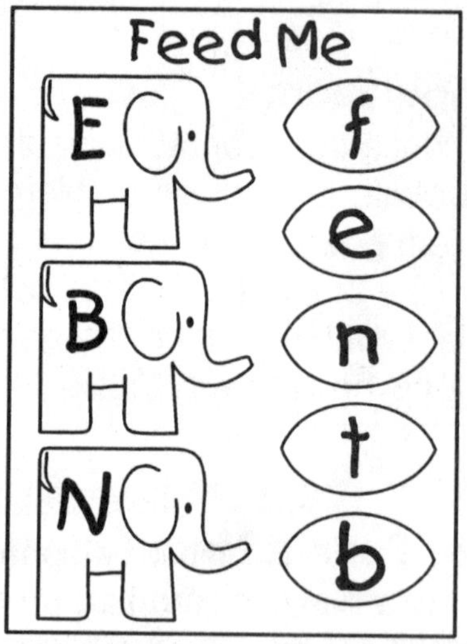

Elephant Phonics:
Reproduce the elephant and leaf form below. Use these to create matching job cards for practicing phonetic skills. For example, make one or more elephants, mark each with a letter (consonant, vowel, blend, etc. - whatever you are studying). Put pictures or words which begin with those sounds on the leaves. Children sort the leaves and "feed" them to the correct elephant.

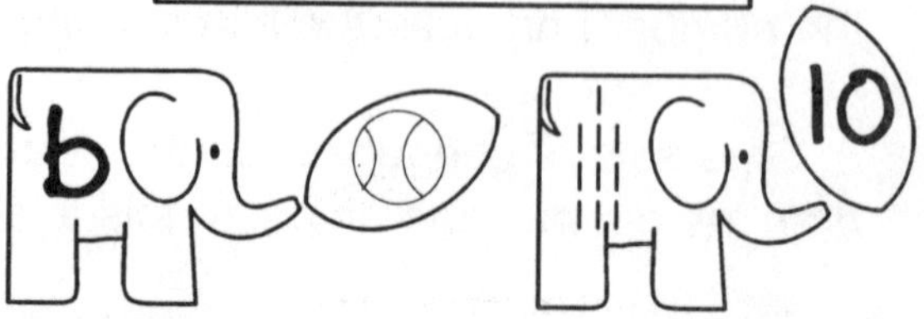

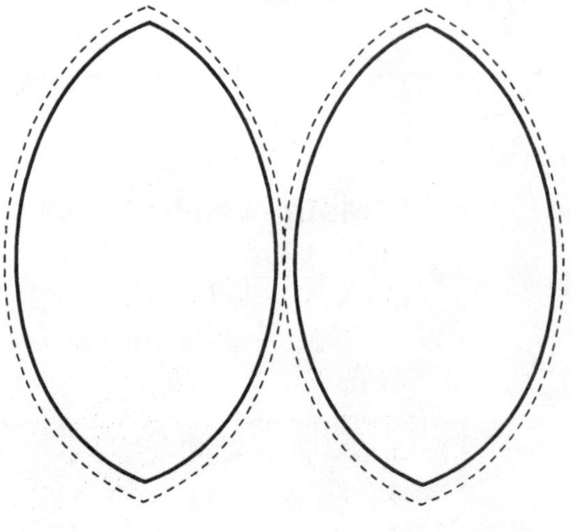

Note: Literature books provide a wonderful stepping off point for learning. This book about fictional elephants is only one of many you can choose from. If it is not available, select another one and set your imagination to work.

Learning through Literature

Read ***A Lemon Yellow Elephant Called Trunk*** by Barbara Softly to your class.

1. **Language - Descriptive and Action Words**
Brainstorm where an elephant could hide. Create a list of describing and action words. Use them to work together as a class to create your own big book. You may choose to use the elephant patterns on page 34. You may want to follow a pattern such as this one...

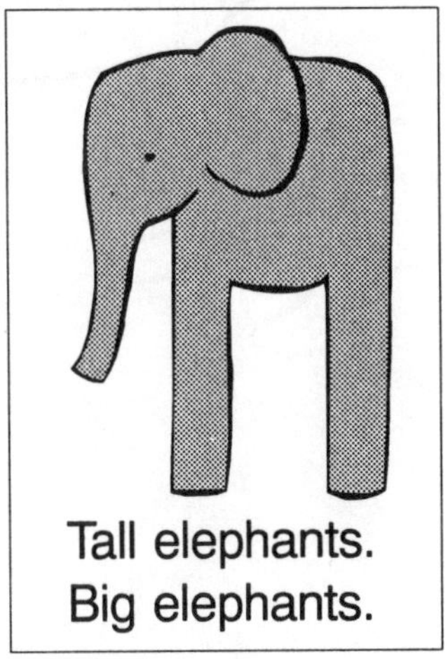

2. **Art - Yellow Gelatin Painting**
Paint a lemon elephant using one package of lemon gelatin mix, a small amount of yellow tempera and 1/2 cup of cold water. Paint with this mixture. The painting will feel rough just like a real elephant's skin!

3. **Math - Lemon Drops**
Make a set of number cards from one to ten. Have a child draw a number, then drop that number of lemon drops into a milk jug. While that child is dropping the lemon drops, the other children are counting. They then write the correct number on a construction paper lemon drop. If they are able, have them print the number word also.

Rainforest Frogs

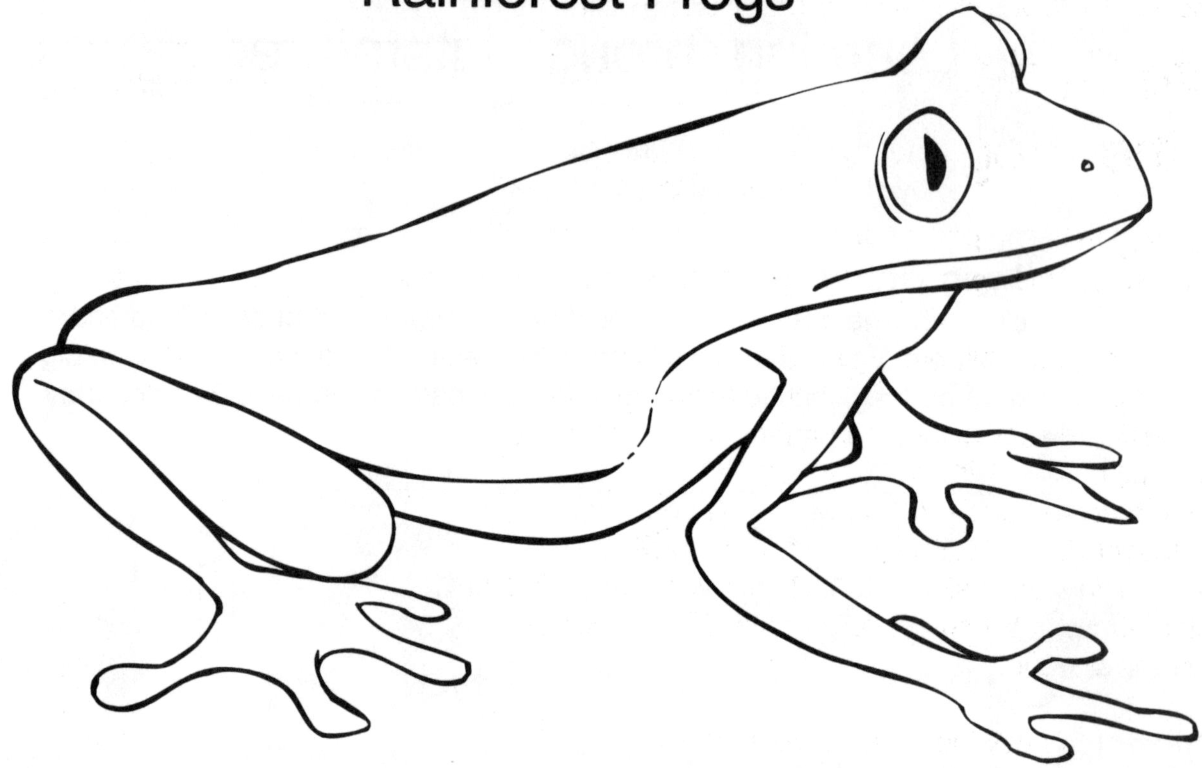

There are many frogs in the rainforest.
Some are big. Some are small.
Some are greenish brown. Some are bright colors.

Note: Children cut out and paste the pictures in the correct order on the "pull-strip." Give each child a 4" X 6" (10 x 15 cm) file card with two horizontal 3" (7.5 cm) slits cut 1 1/2" (3.8 cm) apart in the middle of the card. Children thread the pull-strip through the card to watch the tadpole turn into a frog.

Life Cycle of the Frog

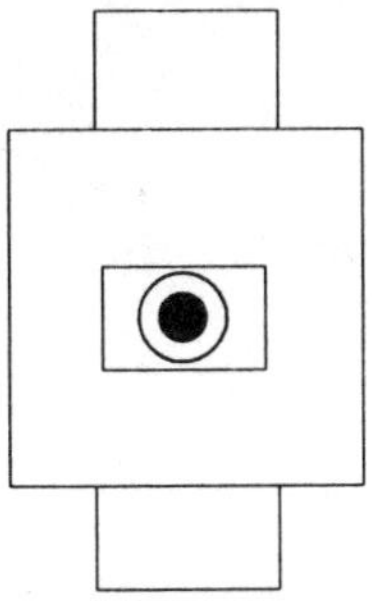

Tell this story to children as they color and cut out their pictures.

The mother frog lays jelly-like eggs which look like small dots or eyes. Soon the eggs hatch and out comes a tadpole. A tadpole looks like a funny fish with a big head. The tadpole breathes in the water with gills which are inside its body. Slowly the tadpole begins to change. Legs begin to grow and the tadpole's tail disappears. While the outside of its body is changing, the inside is too. The frog develops lungs to breathe air with. When it is fully grown the frog will live part of its life on land.

You may want to retell the story as your students lay out their pictures in the correct life-cycle order. Have children check each other before anyone pastes down their pictures.

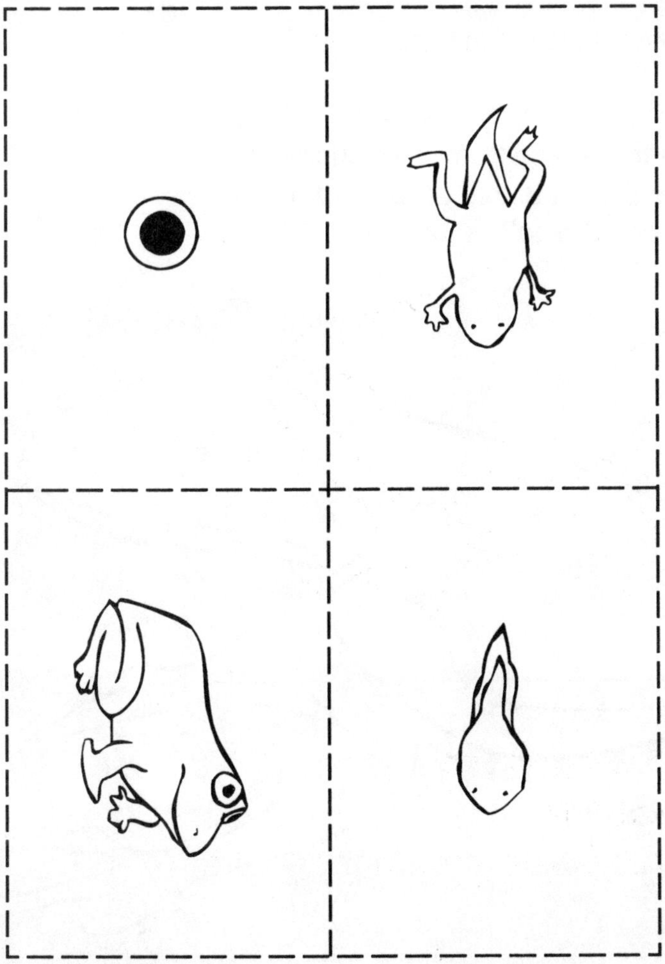

Pull Here

paste

paste

paste

paste

Frog Observation

Obtain a live frog for children to observe. If you cannot find one, use large photographs or clear illustrations.

Have children look carefully at the frog, then ask these questions:

1. Look at the frog's feet. Why do you think it has skin between its feet? *(to help it swim)* We call feet that look like this "webbed" feet.
2. Can you name another animal that has webbed feet?
3. Why do you think the frog's eyes are on top of its head? *(so it can peek out of the water)*
4. What do you think a frog eats? *(insects, worms and small fish)*
5. Feel the frog's skin. Tell me a word that describes it. *(smooth, wet, etc.)*
6. Look carefully at the frog. Does it have ears? Find them.
7. Frogs in the rainforest come in many colors. Some are very bright, others are colored in ways that help them hide from their enemies. What color is this frog? Why do you think it is this color? *(for camouflage)* Where do you think this frog could hide?

Hiding Frogs:

Make copies of this frog pattern. Have each child color his/her frog the same color as the place it is going to be hidden in the classroom. Encourage them to use the jungle decorations in the classroom to help camouflage their frogs.

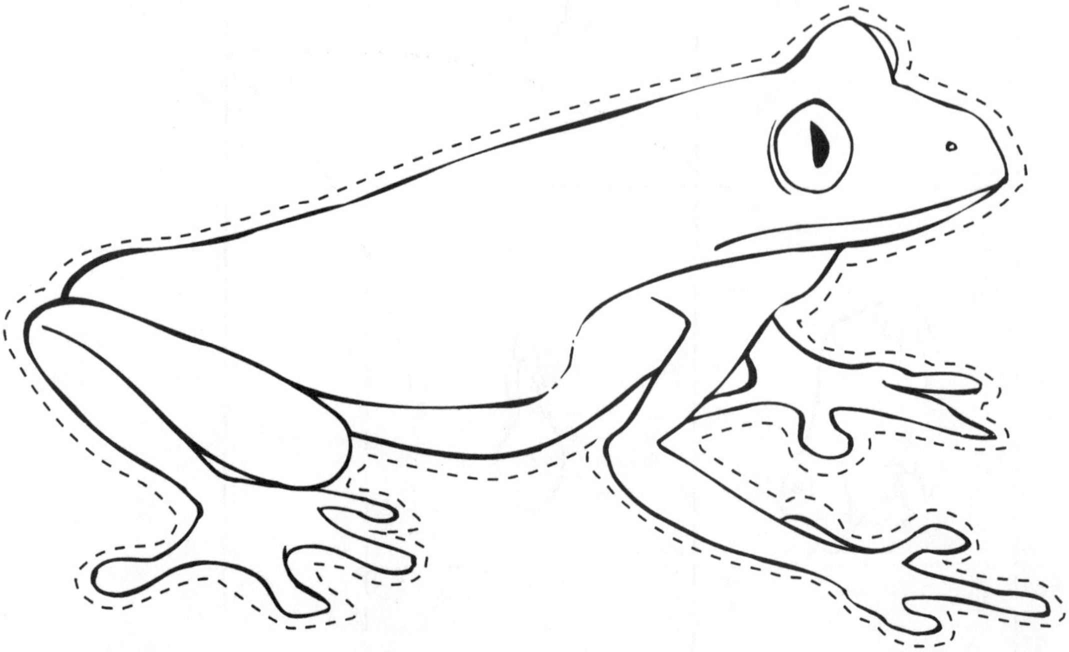

Note: Read ***Jump, Frog, Jump*** by Byron Barton aloud to your class.

Frog Math

Materials:
- lily pad pattern
- green construction paper
- black marker
- number cards 1 - 15

Make fifteen copies of the lily pad on green construction paper. Number the lily pads 1 through 15. Laminate them for longer wear.

Procedure:
Place the lily pads at random around the floor. Select a child to draw a number from the number card pile. The child is the "frog" and must hop to the correct lily pad. (If your children are familiar with the story ***Jump, Frog, Jump*** by Byron Barton they may chant "Jump, <u>(child's name)</u>, Jump" as the child hops to the lily pad. A new "frog" is selected and the game continues.

Variation: Have each "frog" stand by his/her lily pad until all the numbers have been used, then have the little frogs arrange themselves in numerical order. The rest of the class can assist by helping correct any errors in order.

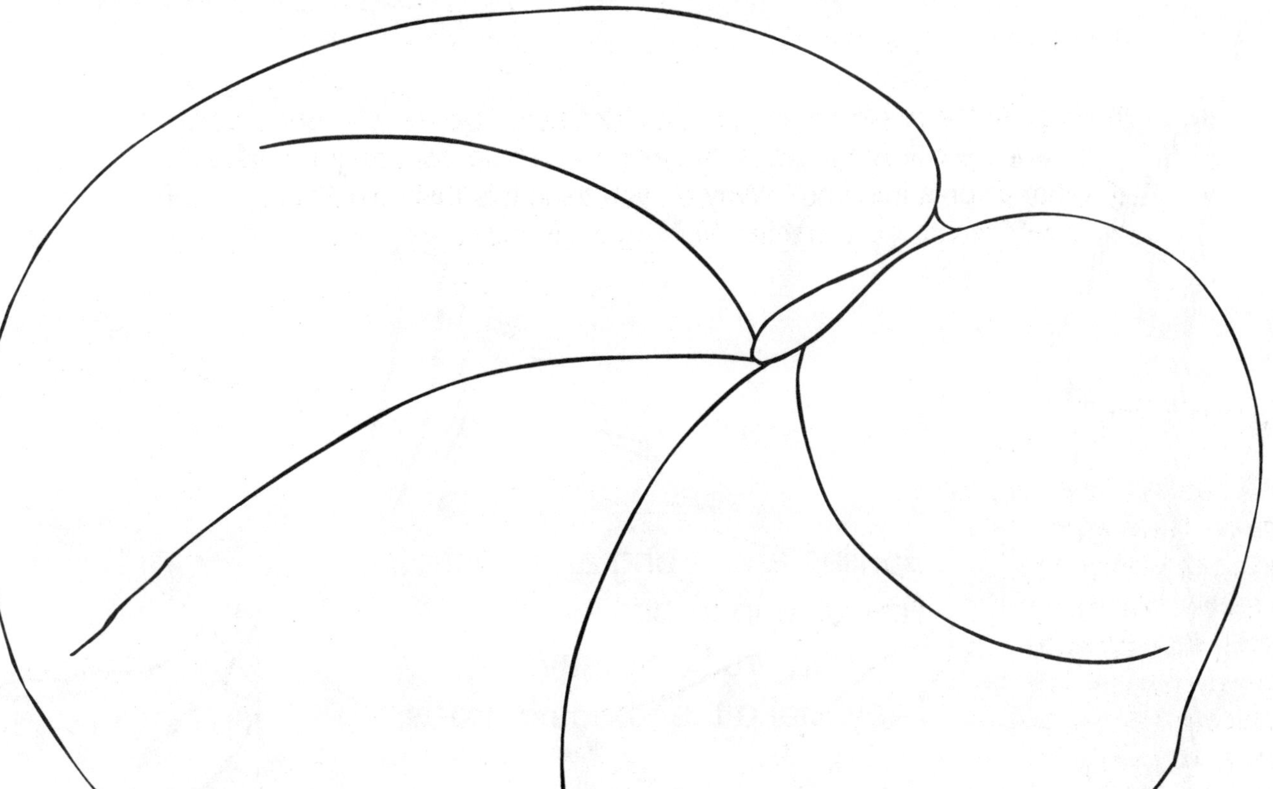

Gorillas

Gorillas are strong and gentle.
They live in troops.
They eat fruit and leaves.
They make their beds in trees.

Color this big gorilla.

Note: You can do these activities with your students even if you do not have ***Little Gorilla*** to read to them.

Little Gorilla Language Activities

Read:

Little Gorilla by Ruth Bornstein: Clarion, 1976. Have your students tell you words that describe Little Gorilla. You may want to record these on a chart for students who have begun to read.

Phonics: Listening for Initial Sounds

Make a set of bananas from yellow construction paper. Put pictures of objects that begin with the initial sound of "g" on the bananas. Include a few bananas with pictures of items that begin with other sounds.

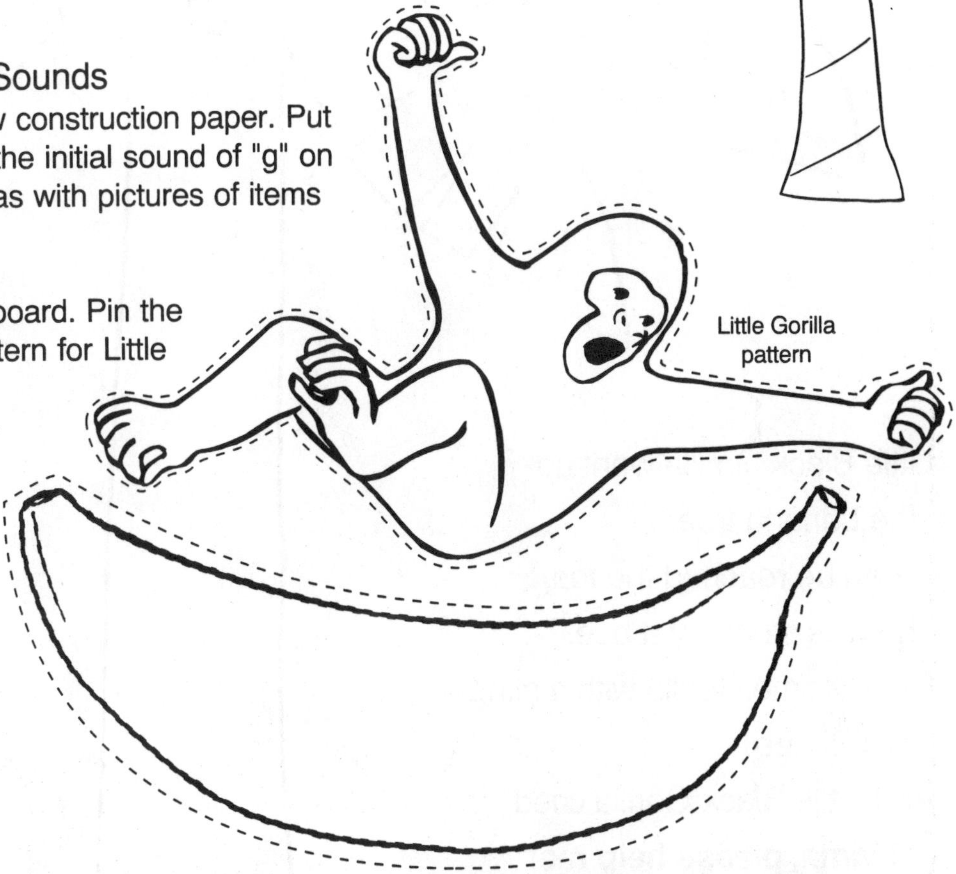

Little Gorilla pattern

Make a banana tree on a bulletin board. Pin the bananas to the tree. Using the pattern for Little Gorilla, make a finger puppet by attaching a paper ring to the backside. Select a child to wear the puppet as he/she picks a "g" banana from the tree for Little Gorilla to eat. Continue until all the "g" word bananas have been picked.

Chant and Pull:

Make Little Gorilla climbing up a banana tree. Begin by making copies of the tree on page 42 and the Little Gorilla pattern on this page.

Ask children to color Little Gorilla and the tree. Cut Little Gorilla out. Tape him to a piece of green yarn 24 inches (61 cm) long. Punch a hole at the top and bottom of the tree. String the yarn through the holes and tie in back. (The holes will last longer if you place tape over the spot before you punch the hole.)

Have children sing "Little Black Gorilla" to the tune of "The Itsy Bitsy Spider" as they help Little Gorilla climb the tree.

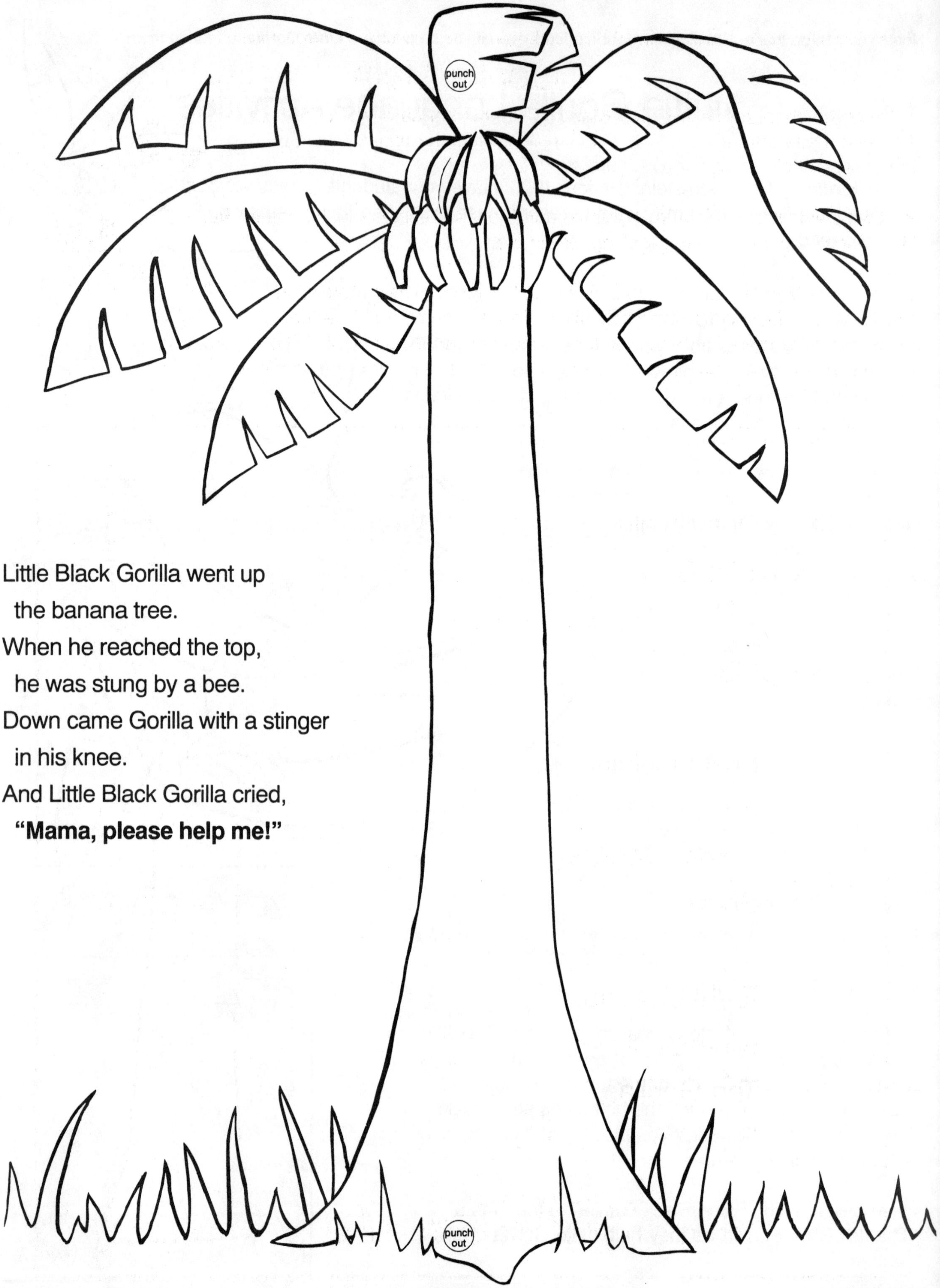

Little Black Gorilla went up
the banana tree.
When he reached the top,
he was stung by a bee.
Down came Gorilla with a stinger
in his knee.
And Little Black Gorilla cried,
"Mama, please help me!"

Note: Teach this gorilla counting rhyme. Color code the word gorilla for easy identification.

Gorilla Math

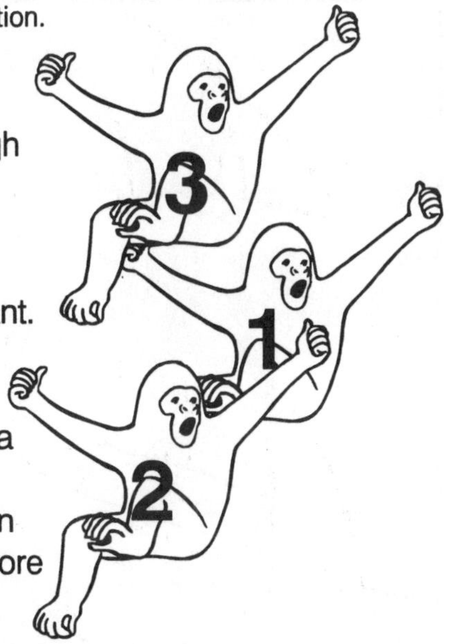

1. Write the chant on chart paper. Make gorilla number cards for 1 through 10 using the pattern on page 41. Have children find the number word on the chart and pin or tape the numeral over it.

2. Have children count how many times gorilla/gorillas appears in the chant. Have them count how many "g's" appear in the rhyme.

3. Select ten children to come to the front of the room. Have them sit in a row to act out the roles of the ten gorillas. As each number is chanted, have one more gorilla stand up, until there are ten gorillas standing. Then reverse the order having a gorilla sit down each time until there are no more gorillas in a row.

Note: Have children clap each time they see an x.

x
One Gorilla,
x
Two Gorillas,
x
Three Gorillas,
x
Four.

x
Five Gorillas,
x
Six Gorillas,
x
Seven Gorillas
x
Snore.

x
Eight Gorillas,
x
Nine Gorillas,
x
Ten Gorillas
x
Roar.

x x x x
Ten little gorillas in a Syc-a-more!

Sloths

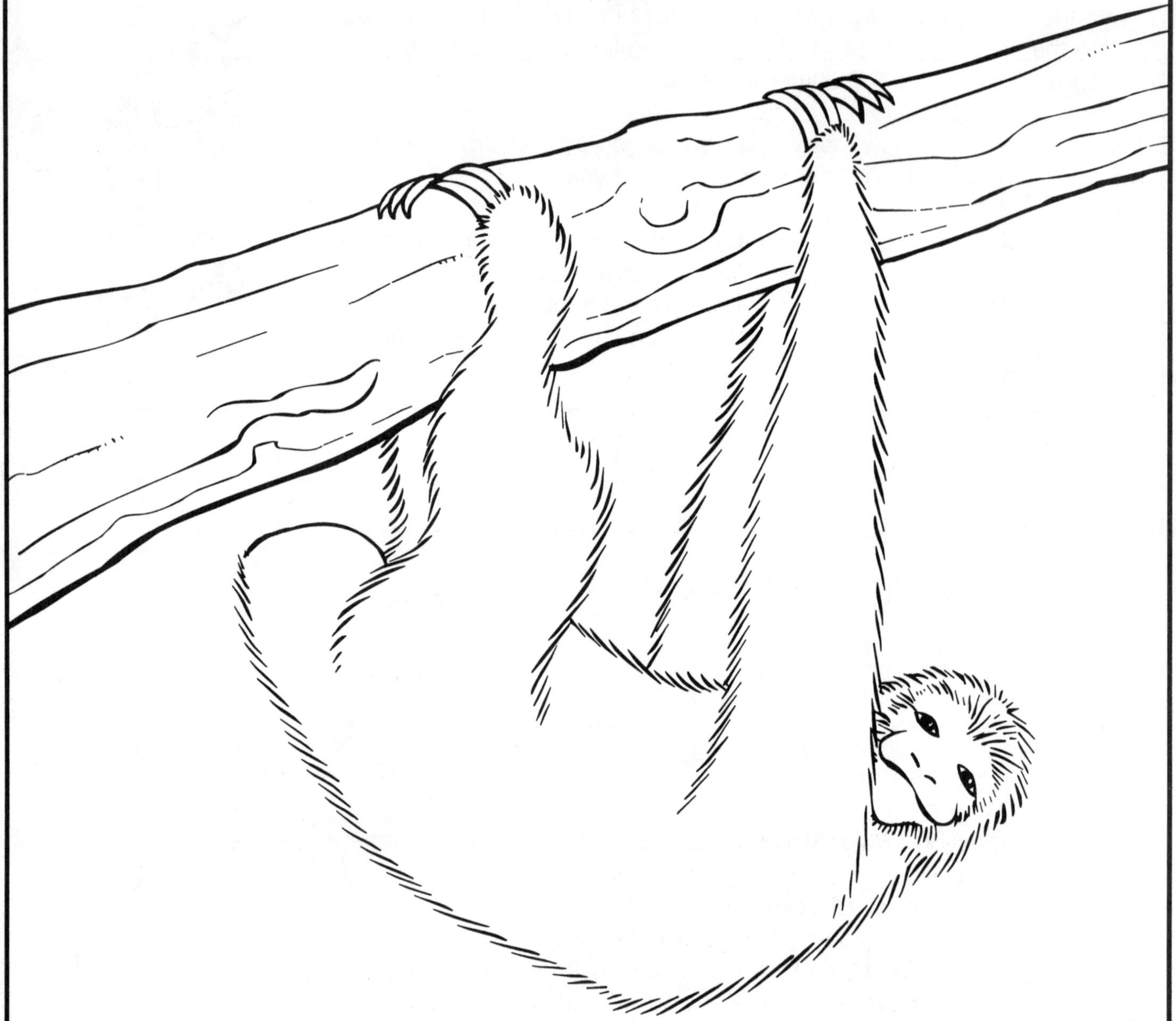

Sloths are slow animals.
They eat leaves and rest most of the day.
They hang upside down when they are awake.
They hang upside down when they are asleep.

Draw leaves on the branch for the sloth to eat.

Note: These sloths can be used for language skills as well as for math. Just change the information written on the sloths and on the trees.

Sloth Math

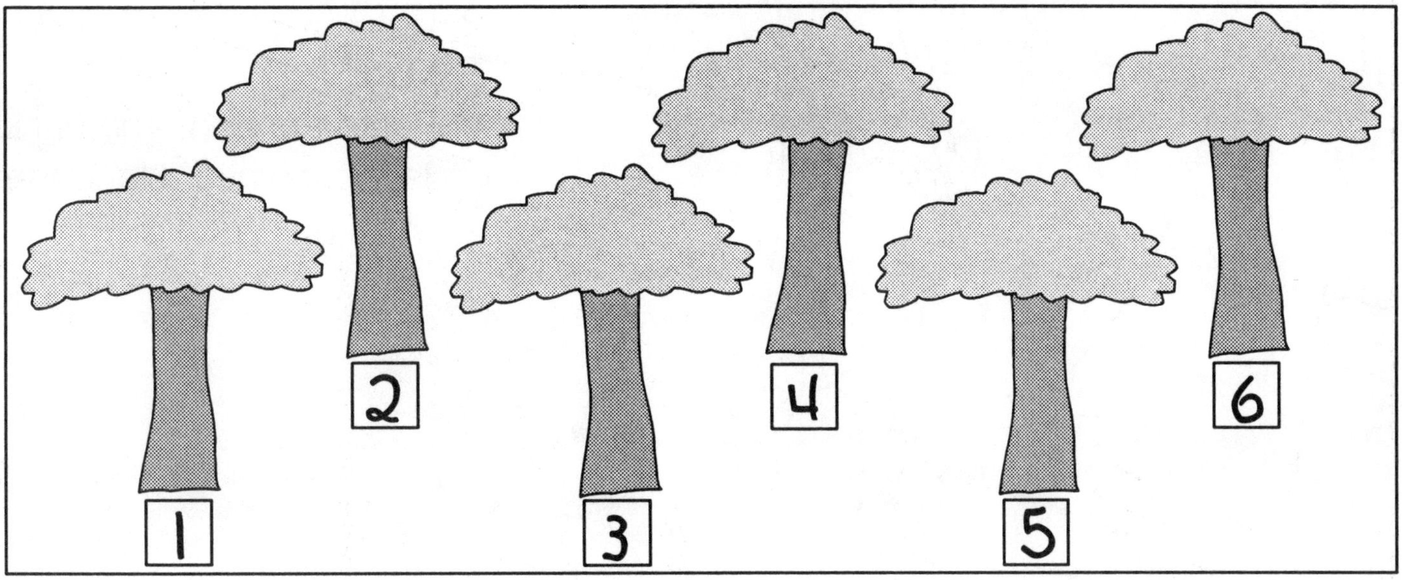

1. Make six tall trees and staple to a bulletin board.

2. Cut eighteen sloths using the pattern below.
   Place one sloth on the first tree, two on the second tree, etc.

3. Cut the numbers 1 through 6 out of yellow paper. Tell the children to count the sloths on each tree and pin the correct number under it.

Variation - Place several sloths on each tree. Pin a number under the tree. Ask children to determine the following information...

- What does the number say?
- How many sloths are in the tree?
- Are there more/less sloths than the number says?
- How many more should we add or how many should we take away to have as many sloths as the number says?

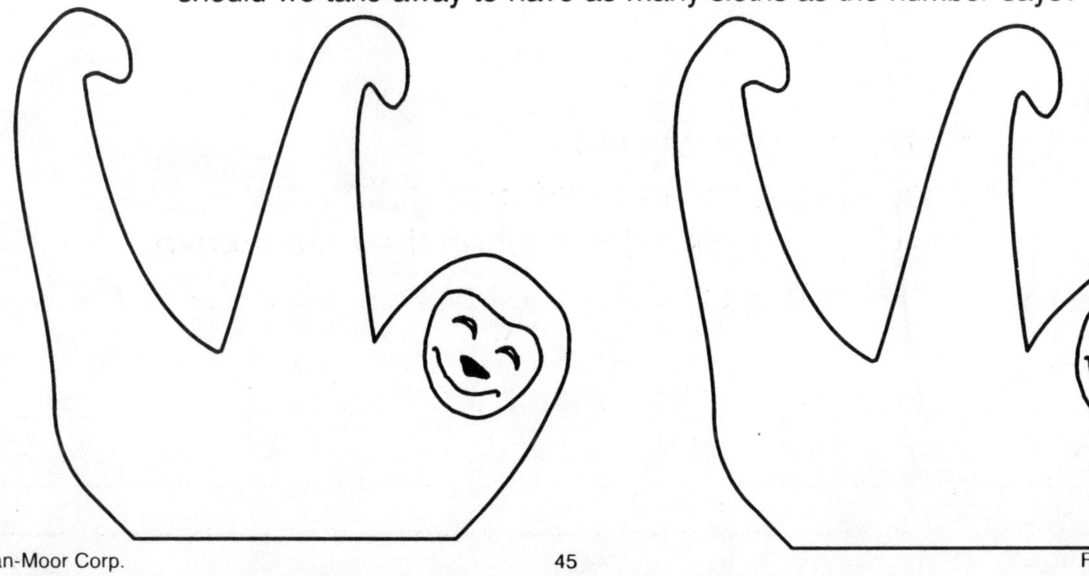

Hanging Sloth Pattern

1. Color.
2. Cut.
3. Fold.
4. Paste the front and back legs together. Hang the sloth on a pencil.

EXPLORING THE RAINFOREST

Activities • Reproducibles • Patterns

Julie Kobylinski

OM WITH A VIEW from COPYCAT PRESS

illustrations by
Jo Anna
Poehlmann

EXPLORING THE RAINFOREST

A WHOLE-LANGUAGE APPROACH

Invite your students into a fascinating new world. Create an exciting and mysterious tropical rainforest right in your own classroom. Set the stage with ideas and patterns to construct an environment of trees, vines, and rainforest creatures. Discover the many varieties of animals living in this jungle home. Learn about the lush green plants that grow in the layers of rainforest. Craft some of the plants, birds, and animals that inhabit this paradise. Understand rainforest terms. Locate the rainforests of the world, talk about biodiversity, and emphasize the importance of preserving rainforests to save our planet. Finally, find out how you can help save the rainforests and make others aware of their value. Use a whole language approach to this important topic and experience something wild...a classroom rainforest!

LIFE IN AN EMERALD WORLD

Nowhere on earth is life more abundant, mysterious, and enchanting than in the tropical rainforest. Found in areas around the equator and between the Tropics of Cancer and Capricorn, rainforests have a warm, wet climate that invites things to grow. Covering just six percent of the earth's surface, the rainforest is home to over one half the plant and animal species living in the world. A typical patch of rainforest (about four square miles) may contain up to 1,500 species of flowering plants, 750 species of trees, 125 species of mammals, 400 species of birds, 100 species of reptiles, 60 species of amphibians, 150 species of butterflies, and so many insects it would be difficult to determine. Many of those plants and animals are found only in that area of the rainforest and nowhere else in the world.

As we study the rainforest we learn how all living things are alike, what makes them unique, and what living things must do to survive. We learn how plants and animals depend upon and interact with each other and their environment to meet the challenges of everyday life. Over one hundred million years old, the forest is like a living museum. Plants and animals that have disappeared from other parts of the world are alive today in the rainforests. The many plants, animals, vibrant colors, and exotic sounds of the rainforest illustrate the magnificence of this tropical paradise.

Layers of life

Rainforest vegetation is divided by scientists into several layers, each with its own climate, special plants, and animal inhabitants:

Emergent Layer

Giant trees that grow to a height of 250 feet tower over the rainforest and make up the emergent layer. The tall, slender trunks of these giants often have interesting structures such as buttresses or stilt roots that help support the tree's shallow root systems. Exposed to the sun and the wind, the tree's leaves are often thick and waxy, helping to retain water. Few animals live at this height, but you may find some types of monkeys, birds of prey such as the Harpy eagle, and the beautiful Morpho butterfly.

Canopy Layer

The canopy, the brightest and airiest layer of the rainforest, forms an umbrella at about 100 feet. These flat-crowned trees, like the emergents, experience changing weather conditions and are often supported by buttresses and stilt roots. Because this layer gets much of the rain that falls on the forest, the leaves of many canopy trees are pointed, allowing water that falls on the leaf to run off. The "drip tips" keep the surface dry and discourage growth of mold, lichen, and other small plants. Orchids, bromeliads, vines, and many other plants are found growing on the trunks and branches of the trees.

Thousands of animals make their home in the dense foliage of the canopy, where food and sunlight is abundant. Here animals such as monkeys and sloths use the branches as pathways. They have developed unique ways of getting food in their treetop homes. Forest birds nest in hollow trunks and rotting branches where they can hide from predators. Beautifully colored toucans and macaws call to one another as they search for fruit to eat. Bats and snakes discover that the trees are a good place to sleep during the day. While the tamandua anteater looks for termites to eat, brilliantly colored butterflies flutter among the branches. The canopy is alive with living creatures.

Understory

The shadowy area below the canopy is the understory layer. Here shrubs, young canopy trees, and woody plants that seldom grow more than 12 feet high can be found. Some of these plants may someday join the canopy while others will always be part of the understory. The crowns of these trees, unlike those of the canopy, look like the flame of a candle. The leaves are usually large to absorb as much sunlight as possible in this dimly lit area. The understory is home to snakes, birds, bats, monkeys, jaguars, and the largest concentration of insects in the rainforest.

Forest Floor

The forest floor is much different than the other layers of the rainforest. It is quite open with a soft carpet of moss and decaying leaves covering the ground. Helped by millions of insects and fungi, the decaying plant and animal materials are turned into minerals needed by the trees to keep growing. Decay occurs quickly in the tropics, where the forest floor is cool, dark, and damp. Ferns and mosses—plants that need almost no light—grow here. Lianas, woody climbing plants that loop through several levels of the rainforest, are rooted in the ground. Sometimes a burst of sunlight pours in from above or a large tree falls, creating a clearing. This spot will soon be filled with low-growing plants and eventually tall trees that will become part of the other layers. Along with the insects, animal life includes toads, frogs, rodents, larger animals that usually live alone or in twos or threes, snakes, and flightless birds such as pheasants and peacocks. The forest floor is a busy place!

RAINFOREST

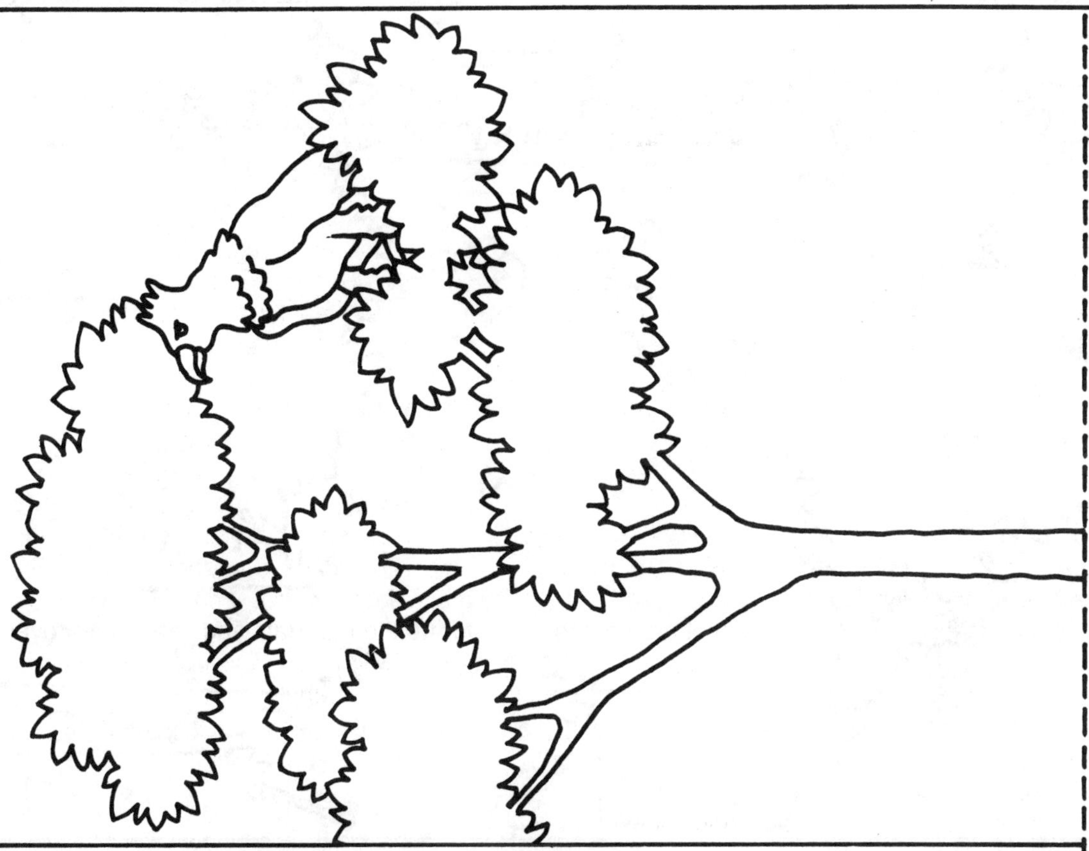

Paste #3 here.

4 Emergent Layer

Paste #1 here.

2 Understory

Reproducible Rainforest Layers

Cut each page in half & paste together as marked.

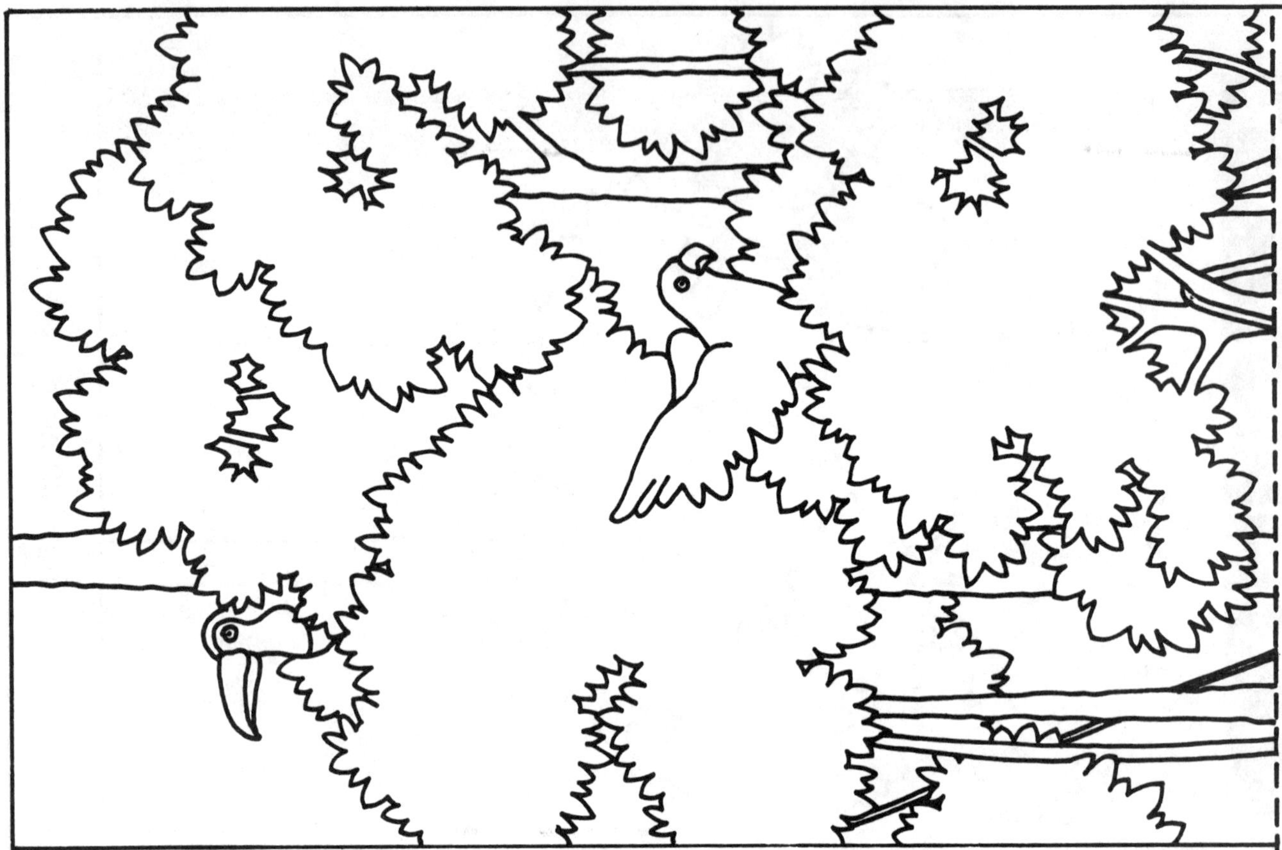

Paste #2 here.

3 Canopy

1 Forest Floor

RAINFOREST ACTIVITIES

Enhance rainforest study with these activities to help kids learn facts and have fun at the same time.

Tropical Forest Prints

Create a special effect with rainforest life using this simple idea. The prints will make great booklet covers and note cards, or just post them and enjoy!

Materials:

9"x12" green construction paper
black printers ink or poster paint
brayer
dull pencil
styrofoam meat tray

Directions:

1. Trim off edges of tray.
2. Use a dull pencil to draw a design (animal or plant).
3. Coat the tray with ink.
4. Press paper over tray and lift.

Tropical Mural

A large mural is an excellent hands-on way to illustrate the layers of the rainforest and its inhabitants. Tape together large sheets of butcher paper and provide paint, crayons, markers, or chalk for drawing. Divide the children into small groups and assign a group to illustrate a layer of the rainforest with appropriate plants. Kids working on the emergent layer may want to draw first because the tall slender trees in their layer begin on the forest floor. Assign other groups to create paper animals for each layer...or add the colorful die-cut animals from the kit. The reproducible Layers of the Rainforest and Critter Cards will be helpful as a guide in creating the rainforest mural.

Giant Rainforest Collage

Introduce author/illustrator Ezra Jack Keats, known for the collage technique used in many of his books. Encourage kids to brainstorm collage materials that might be used to create jungle animals or a "jungle look." Gather the materials needed. Cover a bulletin board with green construction paper and ask each child to draw an exotic plant or animal they might find in the jungle. Elaborate with feathers, fabric, wallpaper, foil, sequins, buttons, etc. Create vines and tree branches using fringed crepe paper, yarn, real bark, etc. Invite kids to help by mounting their plant or animal and adding the special effects to make the bulletin board unique. A jungle collage!

Plant A Mini Rainforest

Visiting a real tropical rainforest may be difficult, but you can see how it works by creating a mini rainforest!

Materials:

clean, dry glass jar with lid
sterilized potting soil
small plants or mosses
gravel
bits of charcoal

Directions:

1. Spread a layer of gravel and then a layer of charcoal on jar bottom.
2. Add 1 to 2 inches of soil.
3. Plant the plants, making sure roots are covered.
4. Water soil so that it is damp but not soaked.
5. Place lid on jar and keep the jar in indirect sunlight.
6. Tissue butterflies or flowers mounted on cocktail toothpicks may be added for interest.

Watch as your mini rainforest creates its own "rain!" The plants inside the jar recycle air by absorbing carbon dioxide and giving off oxygen during the day and then turning the oxygen back into carbon dioxide at night. They also recycle water. To do this, the plants absorb water from the soil and send it up to the leaves. The leaves send the water back into the air as vapor. In the closed jar, the water vapor turns into water droplets. The droplets trickle back into the soil. It rains over and over again...just like a rainforest!

Rainforest Scavenger Hunt

Although rainforests may seem remote, many of the products we use every day have origins in tropical rainforests. Raw materials for familiar products such as cocoa, coffee, drugs, rubber products, and furniture have their beginnings in the forest. After talking about these rainforest products, give each child a list to take home for a scavenger hunt. Ask them to work with their parents to read product labels and find as many items as they can. Gather the tropical treasures and create a classroom display to educate others about the rainforest.

Where in the World?

Post a large map of the world near your display of tropical treasures. Highlight the rainforests and ask the kids to check labels on product containers to find out which products have ingredients grown in a rainforest. Place labels around the map and attach a pin with a string from the label to the area where the product is grown.

Woods

Some of the most beautiful woods in the world come from rainforest trees:

Balsa, mahogany, teak, rosewood, sandalwood

House plants

Many of the plants grown in our homes had their beginnings in the rainforests:

African violets	Anthurium	Dieffenbachia
fiddle-leaf fig	parlor ivy	rubber tree
Swiss cheese plant	Croton	Dracaena
Philodendron	Schefflera	Spathiphyllum
zebra plant	silver vase bromeliad	

Spices

The rainforest has provided us with many of the spices used to make our food taste better:

allspice	cardamom	chili pepper
cloves	mace	paprika
tumeric	black pepper	cayenne
cinnamon	ginger	nutmeg
vanilla		

Fruits

The rainforest is the origin of many fruits we enjoy:

avocado	banana	breadfruit
durian	guava	mango
orange	passion fruit	pepper
plantain	tangerine	coconut
grapefruit	jackfruit	lemon
lime	papaya	pineapple

Vegetables & Other Foods

Some of the foods we can't imagine being without were given to us by the rainforests:

Brazil nuts	cashew nuts	chocolate
cucumber	macadamia nuts	okra
pepper	tea	cane sugar
chayote	coffee	hearts of palm
manioc/tapioca	peanuts	cola
sesame seeds		

Fibers

The fibers and stems of many rainforest plants have important uses for us:

bamboo (furniture,baskets)
jute (rope, burlap)
kapok (insulation, life jackets, soundproofing)
raffia (rope, cord, baskets)
ramie (cotton-ramie fabric, fishing line)
rattan (furniture, wickerwork, baskets, chair seats)

Oils

Oils distilled from different parts of rainforest trees are used for medicines, cosmetics, flavors, and scents:

bay (perfume)
camphor (perfume, soap, disinfectant, detergent)
cascarilla (confections, beverages)
coconut (suntan lotion, candles)
eucalyptus (perfume, cough drops)
palm (shampoo, detergents)
rosewood (perfume, cosmetics, flavoring)

Gums & Resins

The juices and saps from tropical plants are important ingredients of many products:

chicle (chewing gum)
copaiba (perfume, fuel)
copal (paint, varnish)
dammar (varnish, printing ink)
gutta percha (golf ball covers)
rubber latex (rubber products— erasers, balloons, rubber cement, balls, rubber bands, tires, shoes, etc.)
tung (wood finishing)

Pharmaceuticals

Many important drugs come from tropical plants. We have not begun to find the uses for the many plants not yet discovered.

curare (muscle relaxant for surgery)
diosgenin (steroids, asthma and arthritis treatment)
quassia (insecticide)
quinine (anti-malarial and pneumonia treatment)
reserpine (sedative, tranquilizer)
strophanthus (heart medication)
strychnine (emetic, stimulant)
tuba root (rotenone, flea dip)

Rainforests of the World

There are rainforests in many parts of the world. Look at the map below. The dark areas are rainforests.
Rainforests are found in a band around the center of the earth, near the equator.
This band is between the **Tropic of Capricorn** and the **Tropic of Cancer**. Color the band green.
Color the continent where you live. Are there rainforests on your continent?
Which rainforest is closest to you? Draw a circle around it.

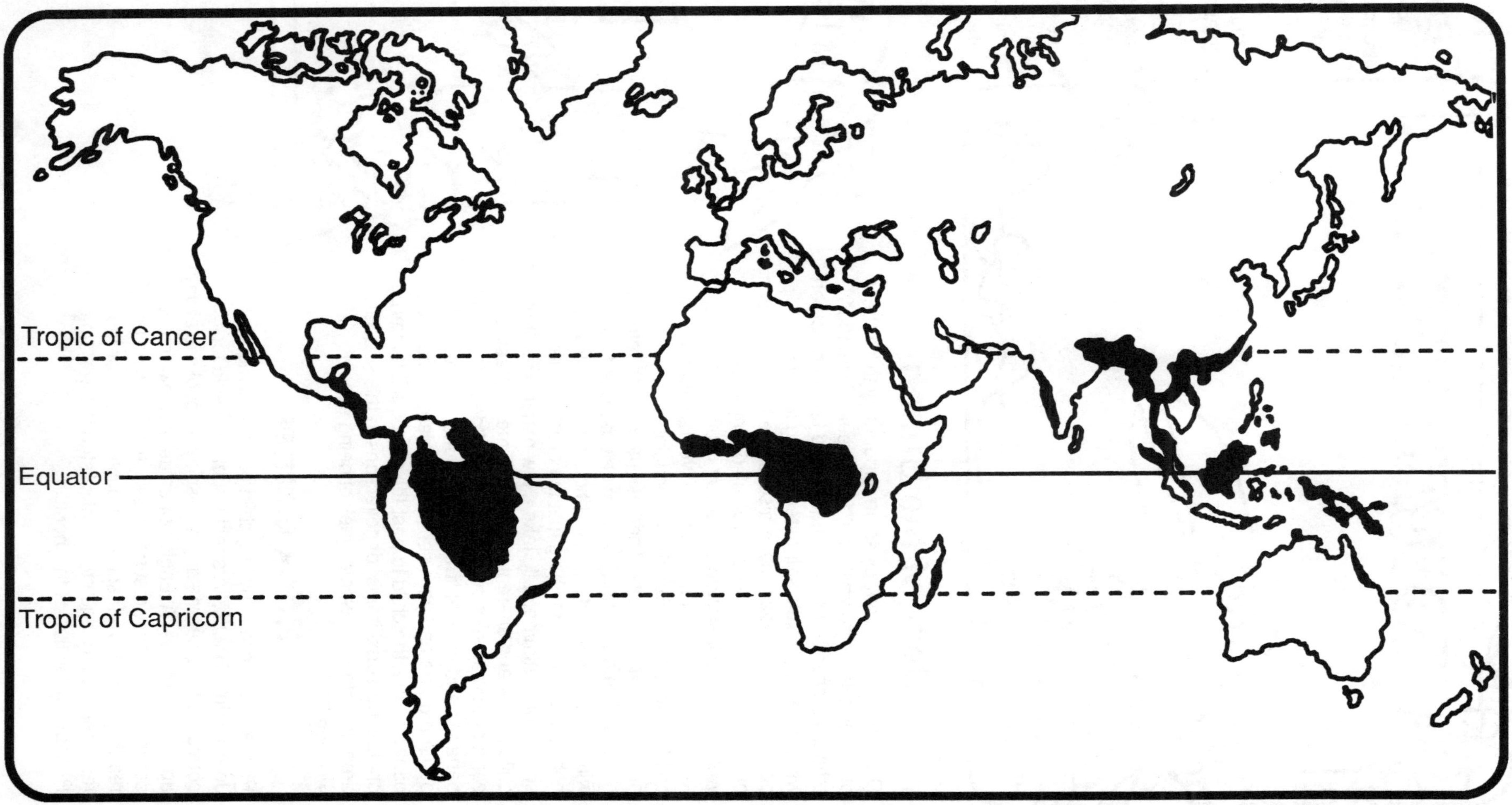

Toucan Times Bulletin Board

This toucan bulletin board is a unique way to display items and articles associated with your study of the rainforest. Enlarge and color the toucan pattern (opposite). Place it in the corner of a bulletin board that has been covered with the classified ads from a newspaper. Add leaves and vines around the outside to create an interesting border. The title "Toucan Times" will encourage kids to use the bulletin board as a newspaper for displaying news clippings, creative writings, or their own pictures about the tropical rainforest. Update frequently to keep the "news" interesting.

Best of the Bunch

Give everyone in your class an opportunity to be "best of the bunch" or "top banana" for a week. To be the official teacher helper, line leader, and featured person will give every child's self-esteem a big lift. At the beginning of the year, make a schedule to assign each one of the children a special week during the school year. Planning it around a birthday is often an easy way to make assignments. About one week before, give the child a "Best of the Bunch" reproducible to take home and fill out with parents. Then ask the child to return the reproducible on Monday of the week assigned, along with items of interest... family photos, favorite toy, hobby display, or anything that the child may like to share about him/herself. Take a few minutes for that child to talk and share items from home. Set aside a corner or small section of the wall and decorate it with bananas and the title "Best of the Bunch." Create a paper banana and yarn necklace to identify your "top banana." Ask the child to post the reproducible, family photos, personal items, or collections in this special area. Imagine… a whole week of being special. Kids will love it!

Book Corner

Plan a book corner inviting children on a "Jungle Journey into Books." A special spot set aside for comfortable, quiet reading or displaying books is always appealing to kids. A jungle hut or just a nook among some of your rainforest trees is sure to lure kids into reading. Check your school or public library for the rainforest poetry and storybooks listed in the Rainforest Resources section of this booklet.

Toucan Pattern

(see instructions for Toucan Times Bulletin Board)

BEST OF THE BUNCH!

My name is ________________________________.

I am ___ years old. My birthday is ____________________.

There are _______ people in my family.

I have ______ sisters and ______ brothers.

Their names are ______________________________________

Family pets: ____

Best school subject:____________ Hobbies:____________

Favorite book: _________________ Song: _____________

Favorite TV programs: _________________________________

When I grow up I want to ______________________________

I wish ____

A CLASSROOM RAINFOREST

Create a tropical rainforest teeming with life right in your own classroom. Or, with the help of other classes, decorate a corridor, a hallway, or a learning center. Make it as large or as small as you like, depending on the amount of space you have available. Fill your rainforest with kid-created plants and animals. Plan interest centers devoted to creative writing, science experiments, display areas, or quiet reading time. Make this a rainforest to remember!

Trees

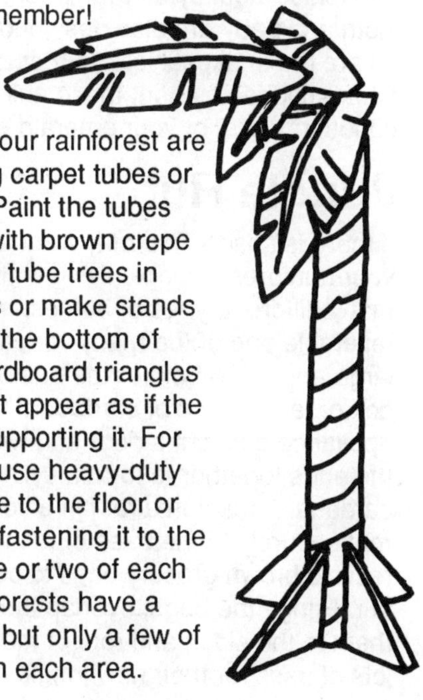

Trees and plants for your rainforest are easily made from long carpet tubes or large giftwrap tubes. Paint the tubes brown or wrap them with brown crepe paper. Then place the tube trees in Christmas tree stands or make stands by cutting four slits at the bottom of each tube. Wedge cardboard triangles into the slits to make it appear as if the tree has buttresses supporting it. For additional anchoring, use heavy-duty tape to secure the tree to the floor or use fishline as a guy, fastening it to the ceiling. Make only one or two of each variety of trees. Rainforests have a great variety of trees, but only a few of each kind are found in each area.

Canopy

A treetop canopy may be created by draping green crepe paper streamers among the tree trunks and stapling or taping them to the ceiling. A more elaborate canopy can be made by draping cheese cloth or netting that has been dyed or painted green and suspending it from the ceiling. Use the leaf patterns given to cut leaves from green construction paper. Or have the kids make their own patterns. You'll need "zillions." Attach the leaves to the crepe paper, cheese cloth, or netting to make an umbrella of leaves.

Vines

Lianas or vines are found all over the rainforest, looping in and out through all the layers. Fat yarn or dead grape vines intertwined among the trees will give this special "authentic" effect.

Bird Nests

One of the most interesting nests in the rainforest is that of the oropendola, a relative of the oriole. The oropendola's nest is a long, bag-like hanging nest. The nests are usually found in groups hanging in the trees. Nest-making can be a fun project for several kids working together. You'll need a balloon, some jute twine (the rough brown twine used for tying packages), Spanish moss or excelsior, and a mixture of watered-down white glue. Begin by inflating a balloon so that one end is enlarged and other end is narrow, with a shape similar to a teardrop. Wrap layers of twine around the balloon, overlapping the twine to create a woven appearance. Leave an opening at the narrow end, where the bird enters. Mix white glue with water in a shallow pie tin. Roll the twine-wrapped balloon in the glue solution until the twine is completely coated. Allow the twine to dry thoroughly—usually several days— and then pop the balloon. Weave the Spanish moss or excelsior in and out of the twine until the nest is lightly covered. Hang it in the tree and position the die-cut oropendola nearby.

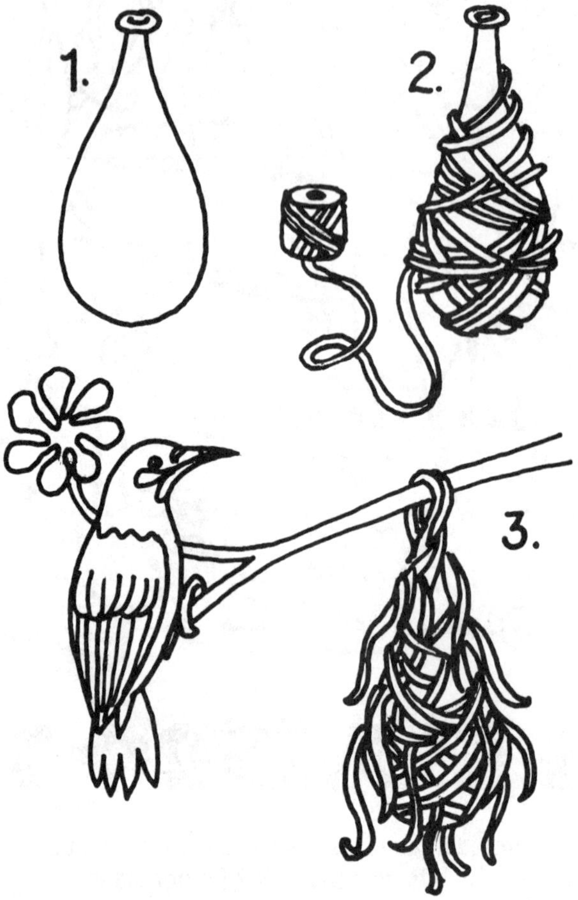

Mushrooms

The rainforest is filled with a variety of mushrooms. After checking an encyclopedia for pictures of different shapes, sizes, and colors of mushrooms, use your favorite play dough recipe to make some for the classroom rainforest.

Rainforest Animals

Once the plant life in your classroom rainforest is established, add the die-cut animals. Hook the tails of the spider monkey and tamandua over a branch. The sloth and baby are also designed to hang from a limb, as are the snakes. Help your students learn a few interesting facts about these animals so they may conduct "tours" of your emerald world.

Jungle Hut

If there is space, you may want to add a jungle hut to your rainforest. People living in the rainforest have many different types of homes, and this hut may resemble one of the many varieties. You will need a large appliance box for the base of the hut and another box or large piece of cardboard for the roof. Open the appliance box, cut a door and windows, and then tape the ends together to form a cylinder. With the additional cardboard, fashion a roof in a conical shape. Attach the roof securely to the base of the hut. Instead of leaves, recycle brown grocery bags to cover the outside of the hut. Fringe the bags, overlap the edges, and then tape them to the sides and roof of the hut. Kids will think of lots of uses for their new jungle hut!

Paper-Mâché Props

Paper-mâché is great for creating three-dimensional props that will add interest to your classroom rainforest. Use your favorite paper-mâché recipe, dress in old clothes, and dig in. What an opportunity for some lessons in cooperation!

Jaguar

This may seem like a big undertaking, but "lots of hands make light work." And the kids will love it! Form the shape of your jaguar by crumpling sheets of newspaper into tight wads and taping the wads together to make the basic form. You can always add a little more paper here or there until you have your large cat and have it in the right position. Then cover the jaguar with layers of paper-mâché, allowing plenty of time for drying between layers. When the jaguar is finished and completely dry, paint it according to a picture in an encyclopedia or wildlife book.

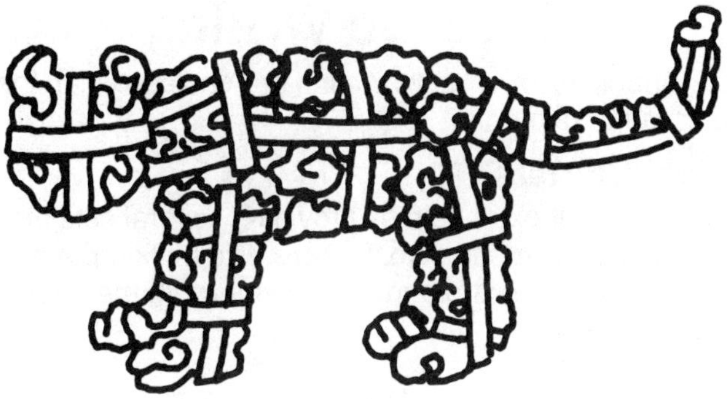

Macaw

The colorful birds living in the rainforest are awesome. Create some of these fantastic birds for your classroom rainforest. For each bird you'll need a L'eggs container for the head, an oblong balloon for the body, folded paper for details, paper-mâché strips, and lots of patience waiting for bird parts to dry between layers of paper-mâché. Cover the egg and oblong balloon with paper-mâché strips and allow it to dry. Join head and body with strips. When dry, add details (tail— paper tube, bend to shape, wings— folded paper, beak— paper cone, legs— wadded paper) and attach to bird with paper-mâché strips. When bird is completely covered with paper-mâché and thoroughly dry, paint it with tempera. Shellac the birds and tie firmly in trees or on vines.

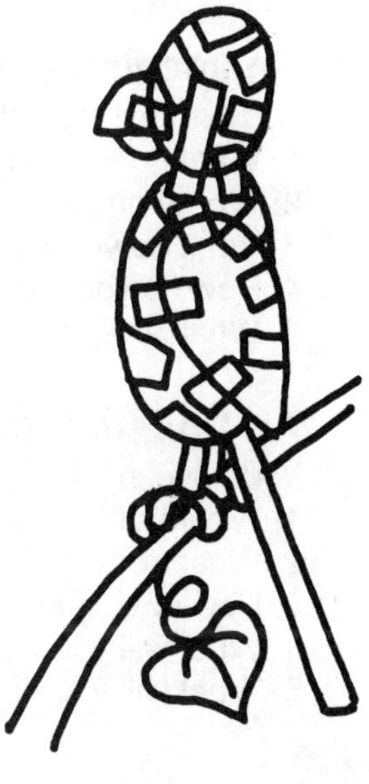

Anaconda

Anacondas can grow to be as long as 30 feet, so you are limited only by the space you have available for display. Crumple pieces of newspaper into tight wads and tape together to form the basic shape of the snake. Remind the children that the snake body may be partially coiled or curved. Cover the tightly wadded paper with paper-mâché strips, allowing time to dry between layers. When completely dry, find a picture of an anaconda and paint yours accordingly.

Termite Nest

A termite nest can be made by inflating a large balloon and covering it with several coats of paper-mâché strips. Be sure to allow each coat to dry before adding another. When the nest is completely dry, pop the balloon and paint the nest with gray tempera paint. Hang it in one of the trees.

Cacao Pods

Cacao pods can be made by covering small balloons with several coats of paper-mâché strips. Allow each coat to dry before adding another coat. When the pods are completely dry, pop the balloons, and paint the pods a light orange color. Cacao pods hang from the trunk and branches of the cacao tree.

Atmosphere

Now for the atmosphere in your classroom rainforest. Give a "real" rainforest feeling by placing live plants on the floor beneath the trees. (Many of our house plants had beginnings in the tropical rainforest.) Hang a bunch of bananas (they grow upside down), some cacao pods, a termite nest, and a few bird nests in the trees. Then invite kids to bring realistic-looking stuffed animals (monkeys, sloths, snakes, birds) to live in your rainforest. Intertwine old dead grape vines among the large trees and place a container of moist potting soil in the corner to give a nice earthy smell. Cover the forest floor with brown (decaying) leaves and turn down the lights. Not much sunlight gets through the canopy. Last, but not least, add a recording of rainforest sounds and enjoy the peace and tranquility found in your own classroom rainforest!

ANIMAL ACTIVITIES

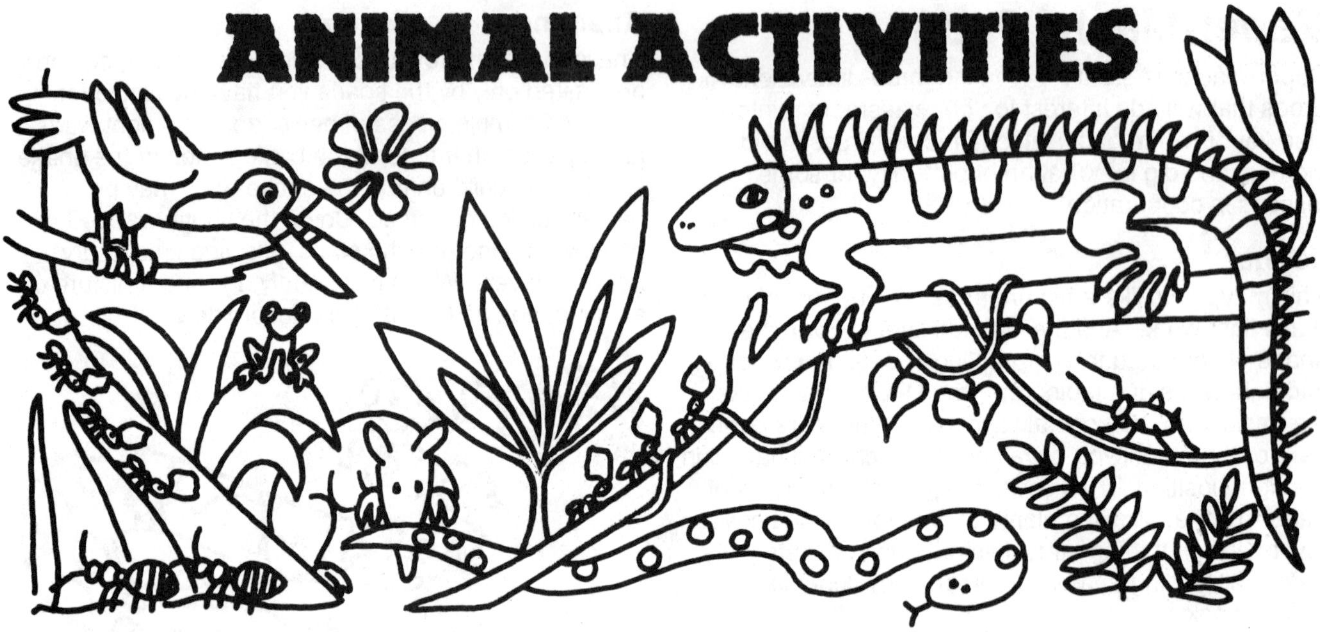

A tropical rainforest is home to millions of animals. More species of amphibians, birds, insects, mammals, spiders, and reptiles live in rainforests than anywhere else in the world. Many have not yet been discovered. Animals are everywhere...leaping or flying from tree to tree, slithering along branches or vines, crawling among the plants, or roaming the forest floor. Some creatures spend their entire lives living among the trees in the canopy of the rainforest, never touching the forest floor. Most abundant of the rainforest inhabitants are the ants, bees, butterflies, moths, termites, spiders, and other insects. The tropical rainforest, with its ever warm and moist climate, is a perfect home for millions of animals.

Critter Cards

Discover a few of the many animals living in the rainforest with reproducible Critter Cards. Use the cards to play matching games, create rainforest journals, reinforce reading comprehension, or stimulate creative writing. Critter Cards may be just the springboard needed to motivate kids to do additional research for reports or oral presentations. The cards illustrate some of the creatures that live in the Costa Rican rainforest. Rainforests in different parts of the world have animals unique to that particular area. Add to your Critter Card collection as kids create their own cards of animals living in various rainforests around the world.

Creative Writing

Opportunities for creative writing are endless when the topic is the rainforest.

Story Starters

Give kids that extra help by providing several sets of story starter cards to stimulate creative thinking. Ask the kids to choose a card and write a story with the help of several questions.

A Bug's Eye View

You are an insect in the rainforest.

1. What do you look like?
2. What will you eat?
3. What is your home like?
4. Do you have any enemies?
5. How does your world look?

An Imaginary Insect

You are an insect that has not been discovered.

1. What do you look like?
2. Where do you live?
3. What do you eat?
4. How do you move?
5. What is your name?

An Unusual Animal

You have just found an unknown animal.

1. Where did you find it?
2. What does it look like?
3. How does it act?
4. What will you name it?
5. What will you do now?

Just So Stories

Rudyard Kipling, in his whimsical *Just So Stories*, was a master at telling "How the Elephant Got Its Trunk" or "Why the Bear Has No Tail." All the unique and interesting animals living in the rainforest lend themselves so well to those same kinds of stories. After reading a few of Kipling's tales, encourage your kids to write their own "Just So" stories. Give your authors a few starters..."How the Toucan Got Its Bill," "How the Jaguar Got Its Spots," or "Why the Sloth Moves So Slowly," and that's all you'll need to create a book of "Just So Stories for the Rainforest."

Shape Books

Shape books always encourage budding authors. Trace several simple rainforest animal shapes, make construction paper covers, and add a few pages of lined paper. Larger books may be used for a class story while smaller books work well for individual writings. Use the books for recording factual information or creative stories.

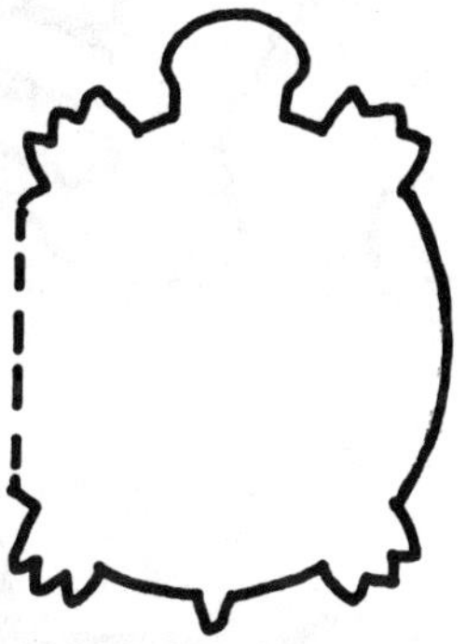

Trace a Shape

Trace the shape of a rainforest animal on a large sheet of construction paper. Using the shape of the animal as a writing line, encourage kids to write free verse, descriptive words, simple poetry, or a riddle following the outline.

Jungle Adventure

Everyone loves a good jungle adventure! Kids will have fun creating their own adventure with the help of some characters, settings, and problems. Take a few minutes to brainstorm ideas... characters, settings, and problems. Then invite students to choose a character or two, select a setting, define a problem, and write an exciting jungle adventure.

CHARACTER	SETTING	PROBLEM
Macaw/Toucan	high in a tree	both want same fruit
Oropendola	nest	strange eggs in nest
Army Ants	forest floor	a slow-moving insect

A Jungle Journal

Scientists keep a record of plants and animals they observe while working and studying a topic. Use the Critter Cards to make a Jungle Journal for kids to record information about animals that live in the rainforest. Fold a sheet of 9"x12" newsprint into four sections. Have the kids paste a Critter Card in the upper left corner. In each of the other boxes ask the kids to write a sentence about the animal and then draw a picture explaining the sentence. This is where the _____ lives. This is what a ________ eats. In the last box ask the children to write a sentence telling something interesting or unusual about the animal. Add the reproducible cover and bind the pages together for a Jungle Journal.

Colorful Writing!

Talking or writing about animals is much more exciting when descriptive or colorful words are used. Help the kids see how easy it is to use "fun" words. Brainstorm a list of animals that live in the rainforest. Then as a group think of words that could describe an animal... brown, striped, shaggy, etc. and interesting words describing movement... gliding, swinging, fluttering, etc. Then take a simple sentence and elaborate by using descriptive words. "The snake crawled" can be made much more interesting with a few colorful words..."The green striped snake slithered slowly through the ferns."

MY JUNGLE JOURNAL

Classifying Animals

Help children begin classifying animals in the animal kingdom using Critter Cards. Ask the kids to place all the mammal, amphibian, reptile, spider, bird, and insect cards together into family groups. Look at the cards in each group and brainstorm likenesses. Then discuss how each group is different. Children will discover "like" characteristics and begin to understand classification in the animal kingdom. Reinforce the concepts with the following games:

Who Am I?

Use the Critter Cards to help children play the game "Who Am I?" Ask everyone to read the information given about each of the animals on the Critter Cards. Then encourage the kids to challenge the rest of the class by giving clues about a certain animal and asking, "Who Am I?" This is a fun way to check reading comprehension, and it gives children an opportunity to use oral language skills to express themselves.

Guess Again!

Here's some fun! Help children learn something about the animals living in the rainforest and check how well they understand what they've read on the Critter Cards by playing the game, "Guess Again." You may have to relax on the noise level allowed, but the value of the game is worth it. Write the name of a rainforest animal on a card—one for each student. Tape one of the cards to each child's back. Then turn the kids loose to try to find the name of their animal by asking questions of other class members. Be sure to emphasize that children are to guess the name of the creature by asking questions that can only be answered with yes or no. No other clues may be given. Do I have a furry body? Can I fly? Do I live in the canopy of the rainforest? I'm a bat! Guess Again!

Butterfly, butterfly, butterfly!

There are many different ways to make butterflies—one for every ability level. Choose the one that best fits your group and then capture the magic of the delightful butterfly by encouraging the children to extend the creative experience. Ask the kids to write a brief description of their butterfly using as many descriptive words as possible. Details might include where the butterfly lives, what it eats, or how it was discovered. Add more fun and write about an adventure the butterfly experienced or tell about how it got its colorful wings.

Create A Butterfly

Not all the butterflies living in the tropical rainforests have been discovered. There are many that no one knows anything about. Ask the kids to pretend that they have just discovered a new butterfly. Then have them record the "find" by drawing a picture of it. With so many beautiful and unusual butterflies living already, the sky's the limit!

Flutterbys

Butterfly patterns may be used to create beautiful butterflies fluttering overhead in your classroom. Use tempera, chalk, chalk dipped in buttermilk, crayon, or cut paper to decorate colored construction paper butterflies. Encourage kids to make unique patterns on the butterfly wings. Then add pipe cleaners for antennae. The more colorful and interesting, the better. Bend the wings to give dimension and hang from above with fishline.

"Stained Glass" Butterflies

"Stained glass" butterflies, although a little more difficult, give a great effect as they catch the light and almost glow. Cut two of the same butterfly patterns from black construction paper. Draw and cut out an interesting design in the wings of one of the butterflies. Place one butterfly over the other and trace the design onto the butterfly below. Carefully cut out the design on the bottom butterfly. Glue small pieces of colored tissue over the cut-out design on one of the butterflies. Then glue one butterfly over the other so that the tissue is "sandwiched" between. Bend wings to give dimension and hang from the ceiling.

Butterfly Pattern

Fold a 12"x18" sheet of construction paper in half.
Placing dotted line of pattern on fold, trace and cut out butterfly.
Use this pattern for Flutterbys and Stained Glass Butterflies.

Biodiversity

Biodiversity is a word that explains the uniqueness of the many, many different kinds of plants and animals that live in the rainforest. Help children understand biodiversity with this reproducible page of butterflies. Give each child two copies of the page. Ask them to label one page "Rainforest Butterflies" and the other page "Butterflies At Home." On the rainforest page, have the kids color each butterfly with a different pattern and color. On the home page, ask them to color half the butterflies with one pattern and half with another pattern, alternating the two kinds. This shows that we may have as many butterflies at home, but that there are fewer different kinds. Ask the children to imagine that something happened to half the butterflies in the rainforest…perhaps their part of the rainforest was destroyed. Fold the paper in half so that just one half of the butterflies show. The others are gone forever… extinct! Now ask the kids to do the same thing with the "home butterflies" sheet. Some of the butterflies are gone, but there are still some of each kind left.

Creative Snakes

Interesting and extraordinary snakes abound in the rainforest. Talk about the patterns and designs found on a snake's skin. Use the snake pattern to help create an unusual snake that might exist in the rainforest. Draw a forest floor or tree branch background for the snake on a 12"x18" sheet of paper. Loop the snake on the paper by attaching it with glue only in certain spots. Ask the kids to write or dictate a sentence about their unique snake.

Super Snakes

These easy-to-make snakes give young children an opportunity to practice cutting skills and have a neat finished product when done. Use chalk, crayon, marker, or paint to create an overall design on a 12"x18" sheet of colored construction paper. Encourage the kids to fill the paper with color and then use a scissors to round off the edges so that the paper is oval in shape. Talk about how the tail of the snake is very thin and its body begins to get larger toward the head. Demonstrate cutting by beginning the tail at one of the edges and then continuing to cut in a circular fashion, with the snake's body growing wider as it reaches the head. Everyone will be anxious to try. When the snakes are finished, add two paper reinforcements for eyes, and decorate your room with super snakes.

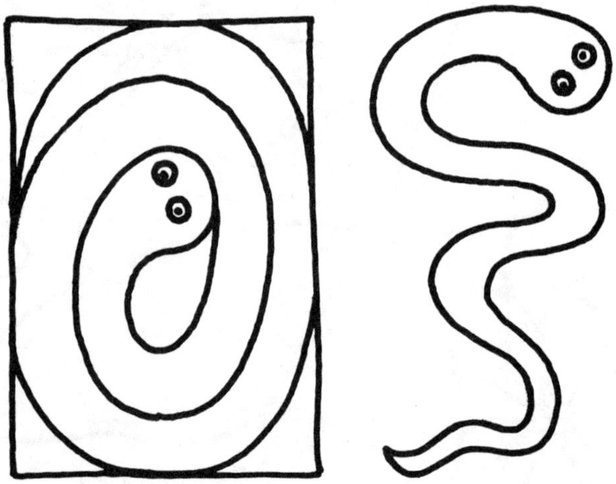

Silly Snake Game

Watch the snake grow and grow as a new child is added in this Silly Snake game. Begin by setting the boundaries of a play area. A large open outdoor playground works best. Next choose one player to be the head of the snake. The head tries to add to its body by chasing and catching another player with its open hand. When someone is caught, the new player goes to the end of the snake and the snake grows...and grows.

Going-Buggy Glasses

Use recycled materials to make some unique bug glasses! Egg cartons, pipe cleaners, and lots of "neat" junk are all you need. Everyone will go "buggy" today!

1. Cut egg cartons so that each child will have two egg cups that are attached.
2. Push pencil through bottom of egg cup, making the hole large enough so child can see through the hole.
3. Punch hole and attach a pipe cleaner on each side of glasses. Twist to fit over ears.
4. Decorate glasses by covering with foil. Then add antennae, feathers, sequins, stars, etc.

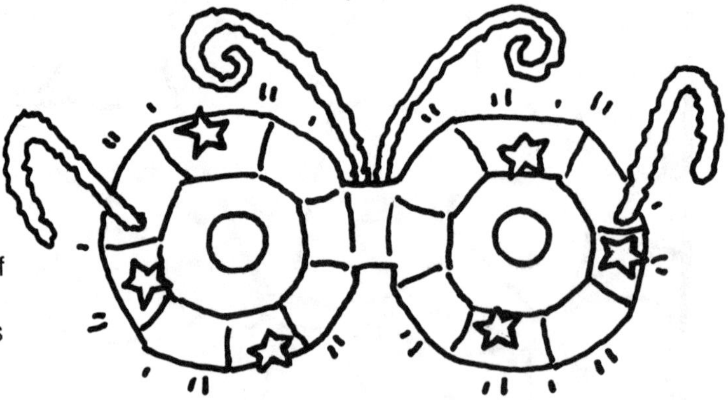

Windsock Parrot

What could be more colorful than a roomful of windsock parrots? Form a cylinder with a 9"x12" sheet of green construction paper. Add colorful eyes, 3-dimensional triangular beak, and paper wings. Bright streamers of colored crepe paper attached to the bottom of the cylinder will dance as the parrot moves in the wind. Punch holes at the top of the cylinder to fasten string for hanging. What a splash of color your parrots can give to the classroom!

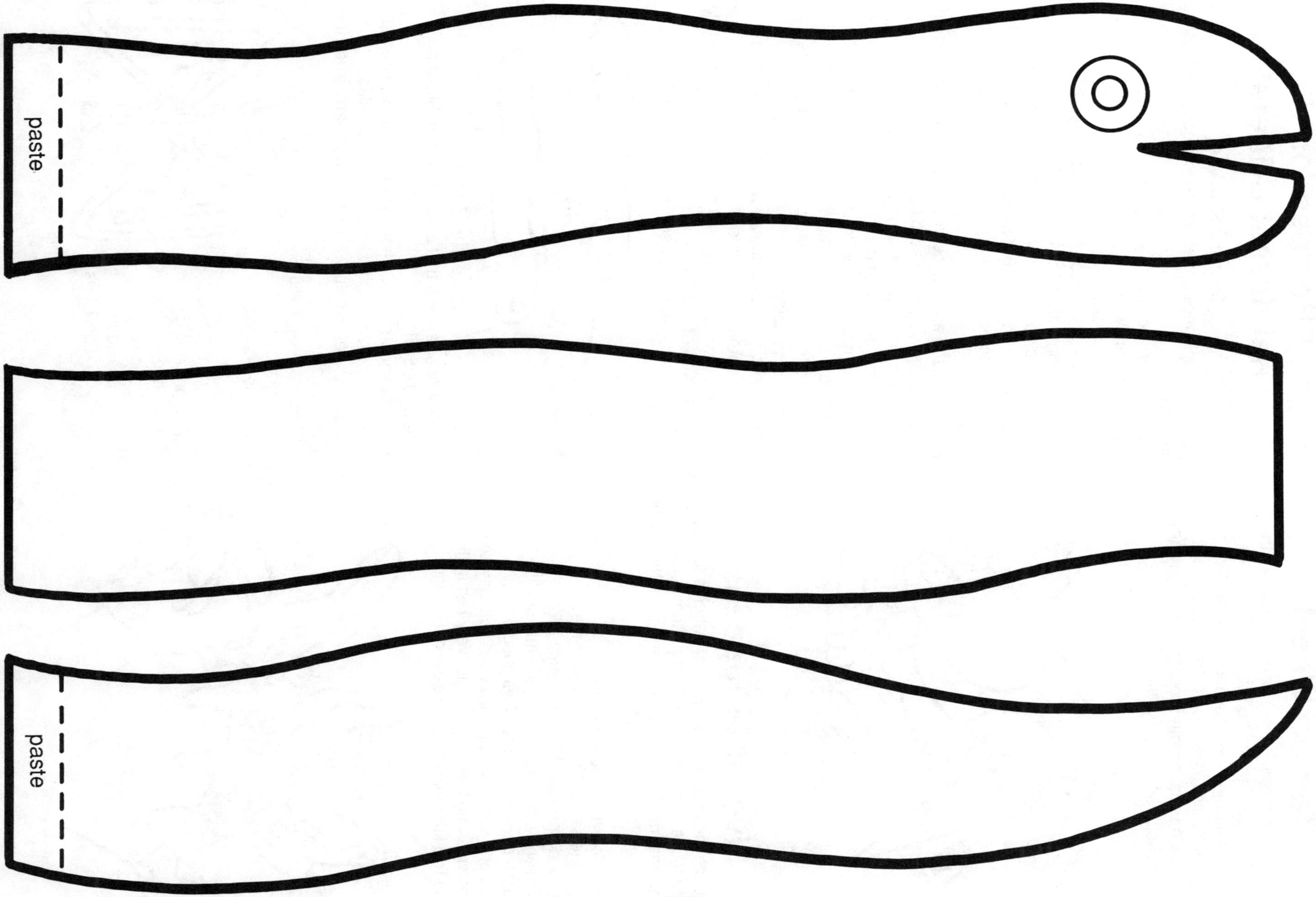

Snake Pattern

Reproduce snake parts on white or colored paper. Use crayons or markers to create a pattern/design on the snake. Cut out parts and paste sections together. See instructions for Creative Snakes (opposite).

Toucan Wheel

It's always more fun when you have a friend like the toucan to help you learn! The Toucan Wheel (see pattern) is an open-ended learning tool to motivate children to practice reading or math skills. Use the wheel for math facts, reading vocabulary, or any new skill. The possibilities are endless.

Five Little Toucans

Reproduce the toucan finger puppet patterns to create five little toucans for each child. Help them color, cut out, and assemble the puppets. Then teach the kids this simple fingerplay for added fun:

Five little toucans sitting in a tree…
The first one said, "Won't you look at me?"
The second one said, "See my pretty bill?"
The third one said, "Your voice is rather shrill!"
The fourth one said, "Careful we should be…"
The fifth one said, "Never know what you may see!"
Then down came the Harpy eagle, very fast in flight,
And the five little toucans flew clear out of sight.

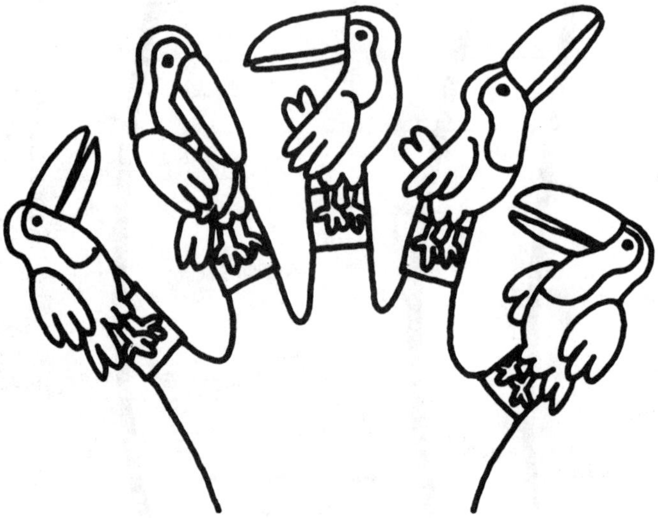

Recipes for Rainforest Critters

Slippery Snakes

Here's a simple recipe that is sure to please the kids!

Materials:

pan, spoon, bowl
self-seal sandwich bags
cookie sheet, aluminum foil, scissors

For each different color snake you'll need:

1 1/2 c. apple juice
1 3-oz. pkg. jello (yellow, red, green, or orange)
1 envelope unflavored gelatin
5 ice cubes

Directions:

1. Heat 1/2 the apple juice in a small pan. Add flavored gelatin and stir until dissolved.
2. Pour remaining juice in a bowl, sprinkle with unflavored gelatin, and stir.
3. Pour cool mixture over hot and add ice cubes. Stir until most of the ice is melted.
4. Refrigerate about 20 minutes until mixture is the texture of pudding.
5. Pour 1/2 of mixture into sandwich bag. Seal bag, leaving corner of bag open.
6. Cover cookie sheet with foil and slowly squeeze jello into 2-inch squiggles.
7. Chill 2 hours and enjoy some wiggley, squiggley snakes.

Butterfly Buddies

Here's a special treat that's nutritious too. Make a butterfly buddy!

1. Spread one slice of whole wheat bread with peanut butter and cut diagonally to form 2 triangles.
2. Use a carrot or celery stick for a body and place the triangles as wings.
3. Decorate wings with peanuts, carrot slices, chopped carrots, celery, raisins… anything nutritious.
4. Add pretzels for antennae, raisins for eyes, and your butterfly buddy is ready as a delicious snack!

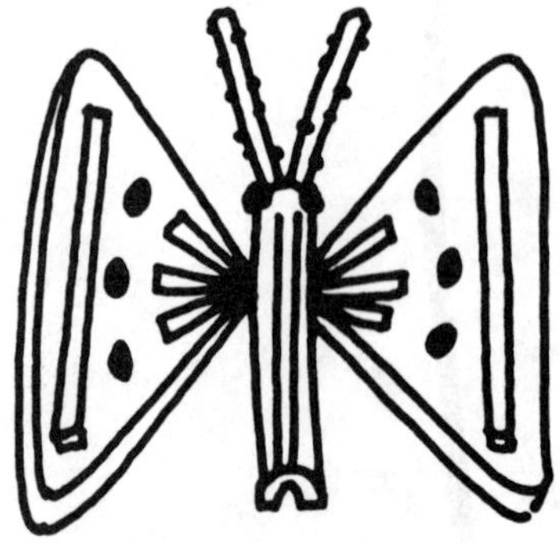

Toucan Wheel Pattern

Reproduce pattern on tagboard. Cut out and color toucan. Cut out wheel and write words or math facts on it (see opposite). Use a brass paper fastener to attach wheel to back of beak.

Five Little Toucans

Finger Puppet Patterns

Reproduce on white paper. Color and cut out toucans.
Paste tab ends together to form a "ring" for finger.

Rainforest CRITTER CARDS

mammal

Two-toed Sloth

A two-toed sloth moves very slowly. It hangs upside down in the canopy of the rainforest. The sloth eats leaves, fruit, and tender twigs. Green algae often grows on its light brown fur and many insects make a home in the algae.

mammal

Jamaican Bat

The Jamaican bat, a mammal that can fly, lives in the canopy of the rainforest. It has a furry body and wings covered by skin. The bat uses its sense of smell to find and eat fruit. It spreads the seeds from the fruit and helps pollinate flowers.

mammal

Jaguar

The jaguar is a large, wild cat that is very strong. Its golden fur has many black spots. The trees in the canopy of the rainforest and the forest floor are home for the jaguar. It is a night hunter and likes to eat rodents and other animals.

mammal

Spider Monkey

The spider monkey has black, brown or golden fur and a very special tail. The tail helps the monkey hang from trees and reach for fruit to eat. Spider monkeys live in the canopy of the rainforest but may be found high in the trees and also on the ground.

mammal

Tamandua Anteater

The tamandua anteater lives in the trees of the rainforest. Its long tail wraps around a branch to hold on. The tamandua has gray-brown fur and sharp claws. It opens the nests of termites and ants with its claws and eats the insects with a long tongue.

mammal

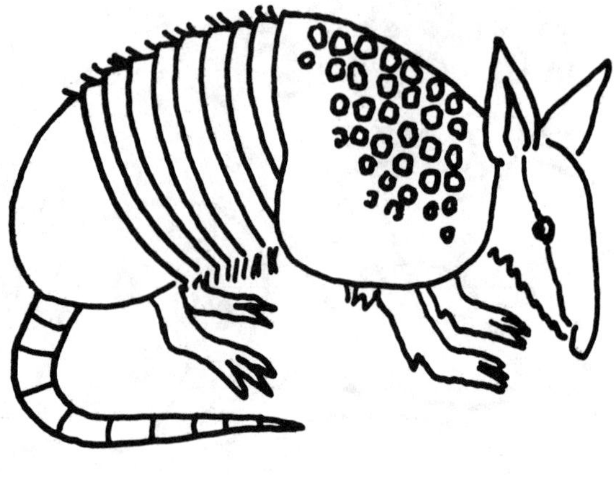

Armadillo

The armadillo's body is a shell made of bony plates. It lives in an underground den. An armadillo digs with its strong claws and finds ants, termites, spiders, snails, snakes, and roots. It licks up the insects with a worm-shaped tongue.

bird

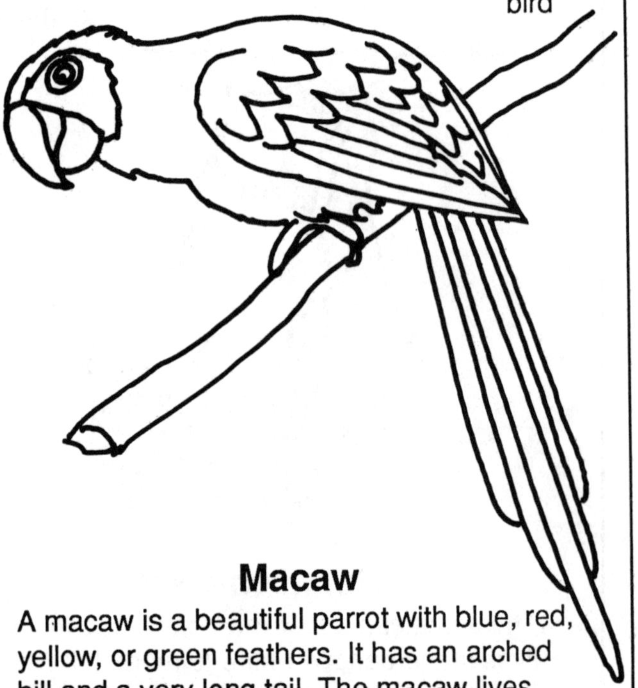

Macaw

A macaw is a beautiful parrot with blue, red, yellow, or green feathers. It has an arched bill and a very long tail. The macaw lives with other macaws. It flies from tree to tree making loud screeching noises and eating nuts, seeds, and fruit.

bird

Paradise Tanager

A paradise tanager is a small bird with black, red, purple, and green feathers. It builds a cup-shaped nest and likes to eat insects, fruit, and flowers. The paradise tanager has colorful relatives also living in the treetops of the rainforest.

bird

Keel-billed Toucan

A keel-billed toucan is a strange-looking bird with a huge bill of many colors. The bill looks heavy but air pockets make it light. The saw-like edges of the bill slice fruit to eat. The toucan lives in a flock and sleeps with its big bill resting on its back.

bird

Hummingbird

A hummingbird is one of the smallest and most colorful birds. Its wings make a humming sound as it darts quickly forward, backward, and sideways in the rainforest. The hummingbird's long slender bill sucks nectar from flowers.

bird

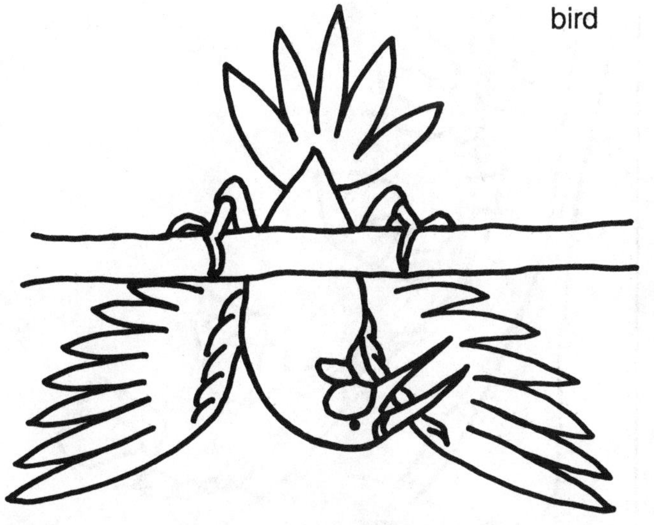

Oropendola

Oropendolas are birds that like to hang upside down. They live in large flocks and build long hanging nests in the trees. Oropendolas eat soft fruit and drink nectar. Sometimes a cowbird puts its eggs in the oropendola's nest and the oropendola becomes a baby-sitter.

insect

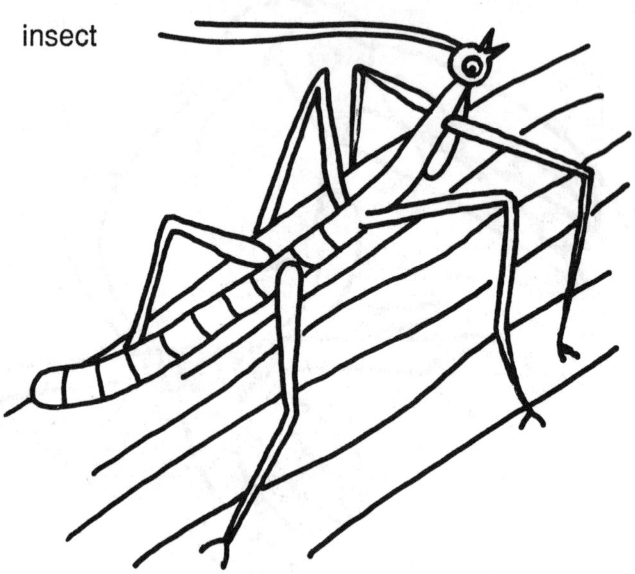

Walking Stick

The walking stick is an insect with a long body, six legs that are all the same size, and no wings. It is brown and looks like a stick. This protects it from enemies. The walking stick eats leaves and as it grows, it sheds its skin.

insect

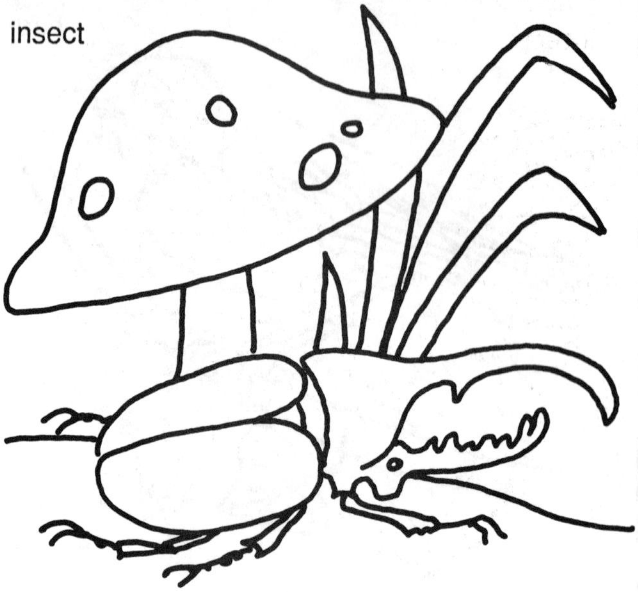

Beetle

Beetles are one of the largest groups of insects that live in the rainforest. Tough, brightly colored front wings protect the underwings that are used for flying. Beetles have strong jaws for chewing leaves and fruit. Some beetles grow to be giant-sized.

insect

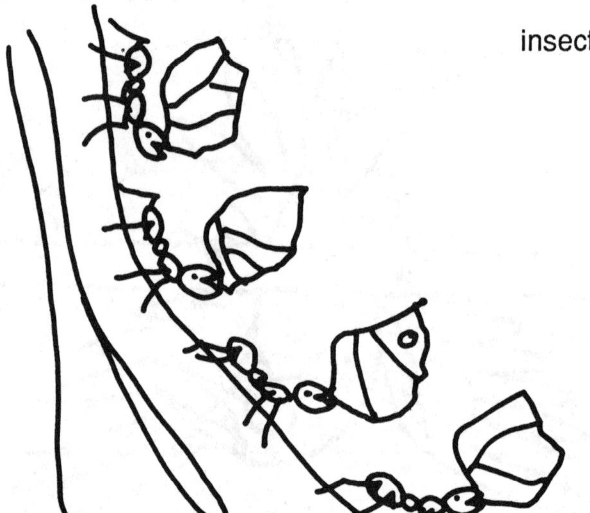

Leafcutter Ant

Leafcutter ants are the farmers of the rainforest. These red ants cut pieces of leaves and carry them like umbrellas over their heads. They walk in a long line to their underground nest. In the nest, they chew up the leaves and grow fungus to eat.

insect

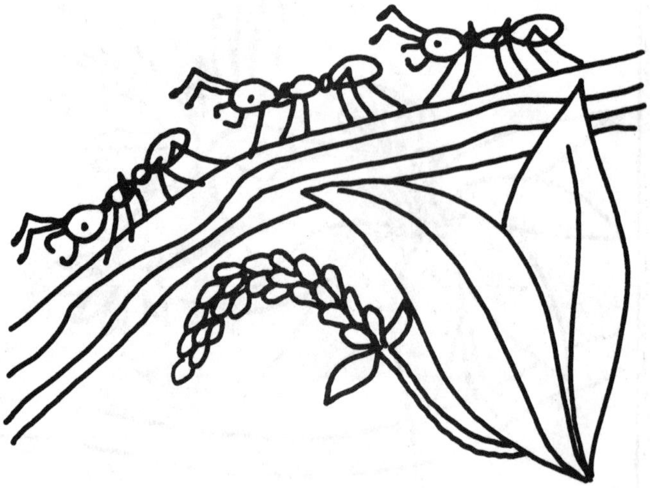

Army Ant

Army ants move in long columns around the floor of the rainforest. Slow moving insects or animals hurry to get out of the way because they may be eaten by the fast moving ants. Army ants make a nest by clinging together in a large ball.

insect

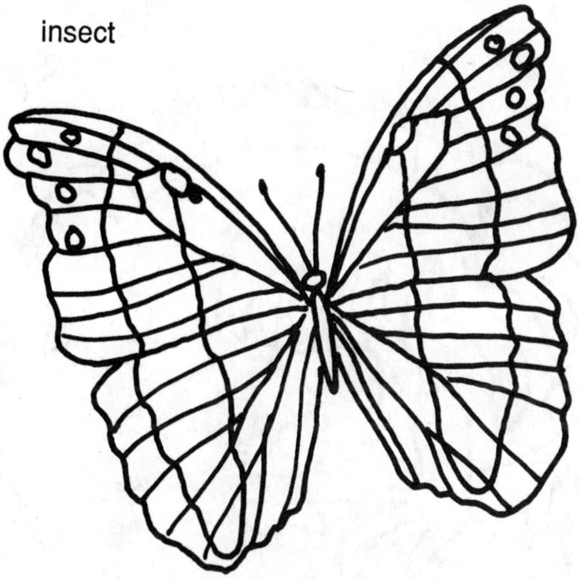

Morpho Butterfly

Morpho butterflies are large, beautiful butterflies. Their sparkling blue wings flash in the sunlight as they fly through the clearings in the canopy of the rainforest. Morphos flutter from flower to flower drinking nectar.

insect

Moth

Many kinds of moths fly at night in the rainforest. The body of the moth is short, furry, and plump. Its antennae are often feathery. Some moths have colorful wings. They use their sense of smell to find flowers and then drink the nectar.

insect

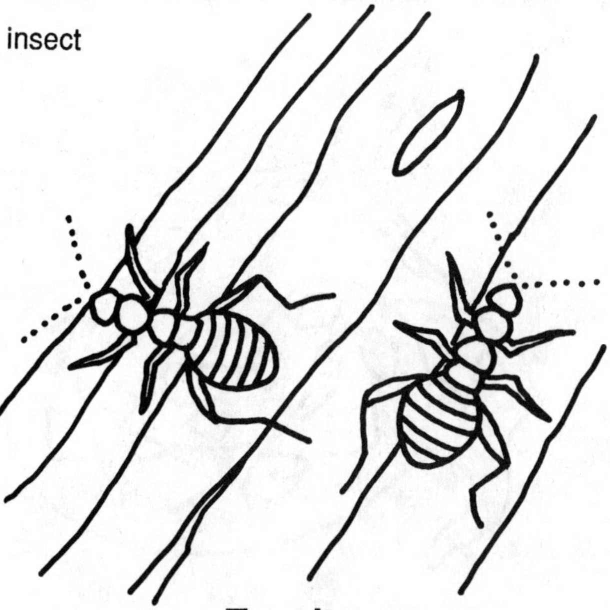

Termites

Termites are small insects that are found everywhere in the rainforest. They live together in colonies and eat wood. Termites build large nests in trees or huge mounds on the ground. These mounds are often taller than a man.

reptile

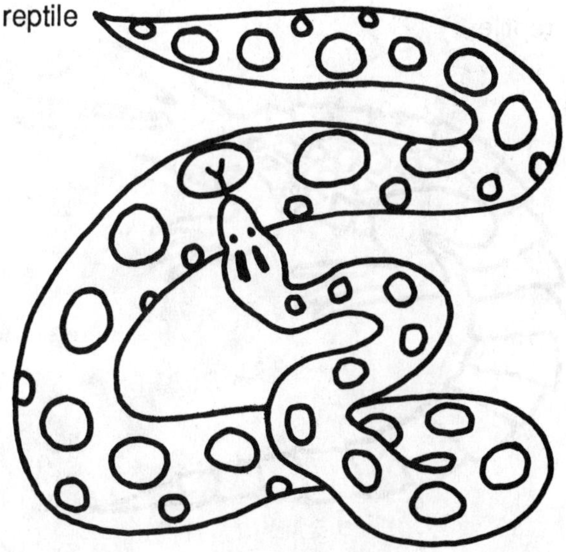

Anaconda

An anaconda is a very large olive green colored snake. It has two black stripes on its head and black spots along its back. This slow moving snake lives near the water and catches birds and small animals that come to drink.

reptile

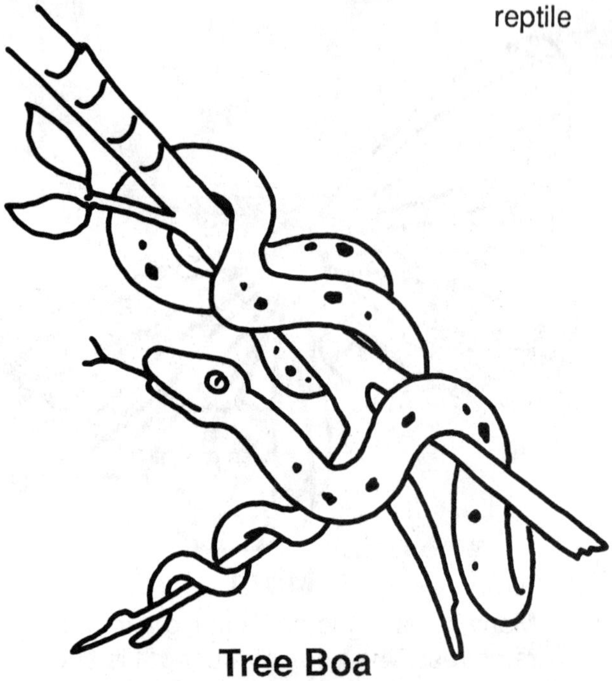

Tree Boa

A tree boa is an orange snake. It spends its days coiled and sleeping in a tree. At night this slow-moving snake hunts and eats lizards, birds, and small mammals.

reptile

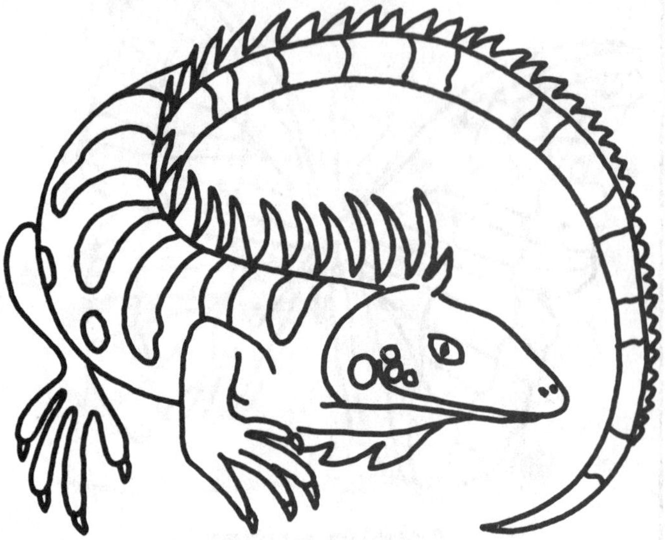

Iguana

The iguana is a large green lizard that lives in the trees of the rainforest. It eats insects and can grow as long as six and one-half feet, including its long banded tail. A large flap of skin hangs from the iguana's throat.

reptile

Caimen

The caimen is a reptile that looks like an alligator. It can be seen sunning itself along river banks or swimming in streams. The caimen moves very fast and has many sharp pointed teeth. It catches and eats water birds, mammals, amphibians, and other reptiles.

reptile

Fer-de-Lance

The fer-de-lance is a poisonous snake that lives mostly on the ground in the rainforest. It is a dark brown-gray color with a black-edged diamond pattern on its back. It has long sharp fangs and eats small animals, lizards, frogs, and rodents.

reptile

Anole Lizard

The anole lizard is a small green lizard that lives in the trees and eats fruit and insects. It has a thin body and a very long whip like tail. The lizard's sharp claws and the sticky pads on the ends of its long toes make it a good climber.

reptile

Ornate Wood Turtle

The ornate wood turtle is a reptile with colorful markings on its shell. It lives on the floor of the rainforest and likes to bury itself in the soft soil. The wood turtle eats insects.

reptile

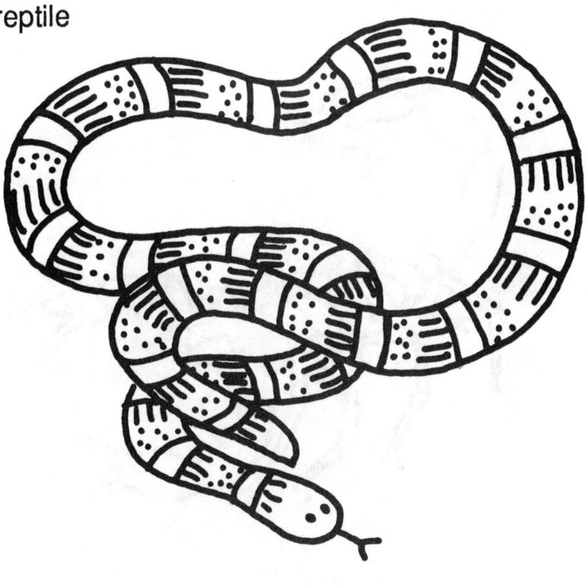

False Coral Snake

The false coral snake has a pattern of coral and dark green rings around its long, thin body. It lives in the trees of the rainforest and rests during the day. At night it hunts small lizards, other snakes, and insects.

amphibian

Red-eyed Tree Frog

The small red-eyed tree frog lives in the trees and shrubs of the rainforest. It leaps from tree to tree looking for insects to eat. Sticky pads on its long toes make the tree frog a good climber.

amphibian

Poison Arrow Frog

The poison arrow frog has a brightly colored body. The bright colors warn other animals that it is poison. The frog makes its home in trees or on the floor of the rainforest. It eats insects.

amphibian

Horned Frog

The horned frog is large with a big head and a wide mouth. Its body is covered with colorful patterns and flaps of skin that look like horns. Hiding in the soft ground, the horned frog leaps out to eat insects, frogs, lizards, and snakes.

spider

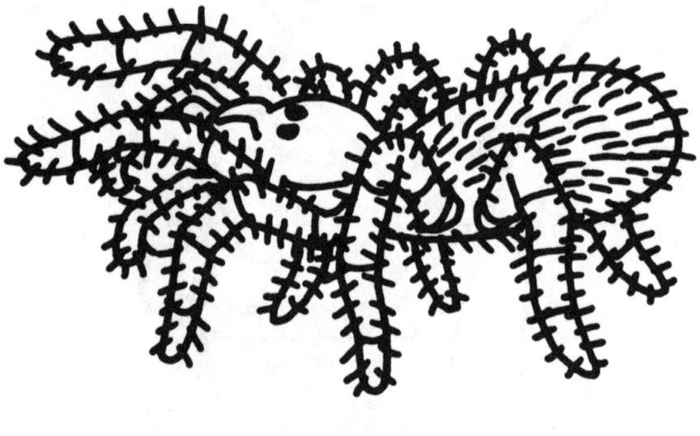

Tarantula

A tarantula is a large hairy spider that lives in the trees of the rainforest. It hunts at night and eats insects. Sometimes it eats small birds. Tarantulas can live to be 20 years old. Their bite is not poisonous to people.

spider

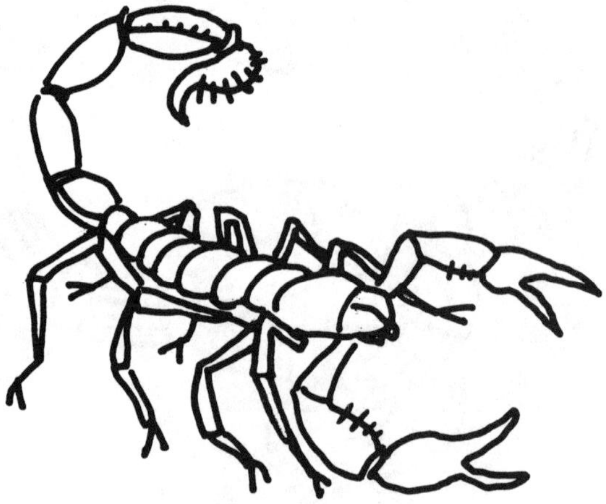

Scorpion

The scorpion is a member of the spider family. It has a long tail that gives a dangerous, poisonous sting. The scorpion lives in the trees of the rainforest and is most active at night. It eats large insects and other spiders.

Toucan Mask Pattern

Cut out and trace pattern pieces on paper plate as shown. Color with crayon, paint, or markers. Cut out beak and eye holes. Fold beak in half and glue tip of beak as marked. Glue or staple beak to mask. Attach yarn or string tie to each side of mask.

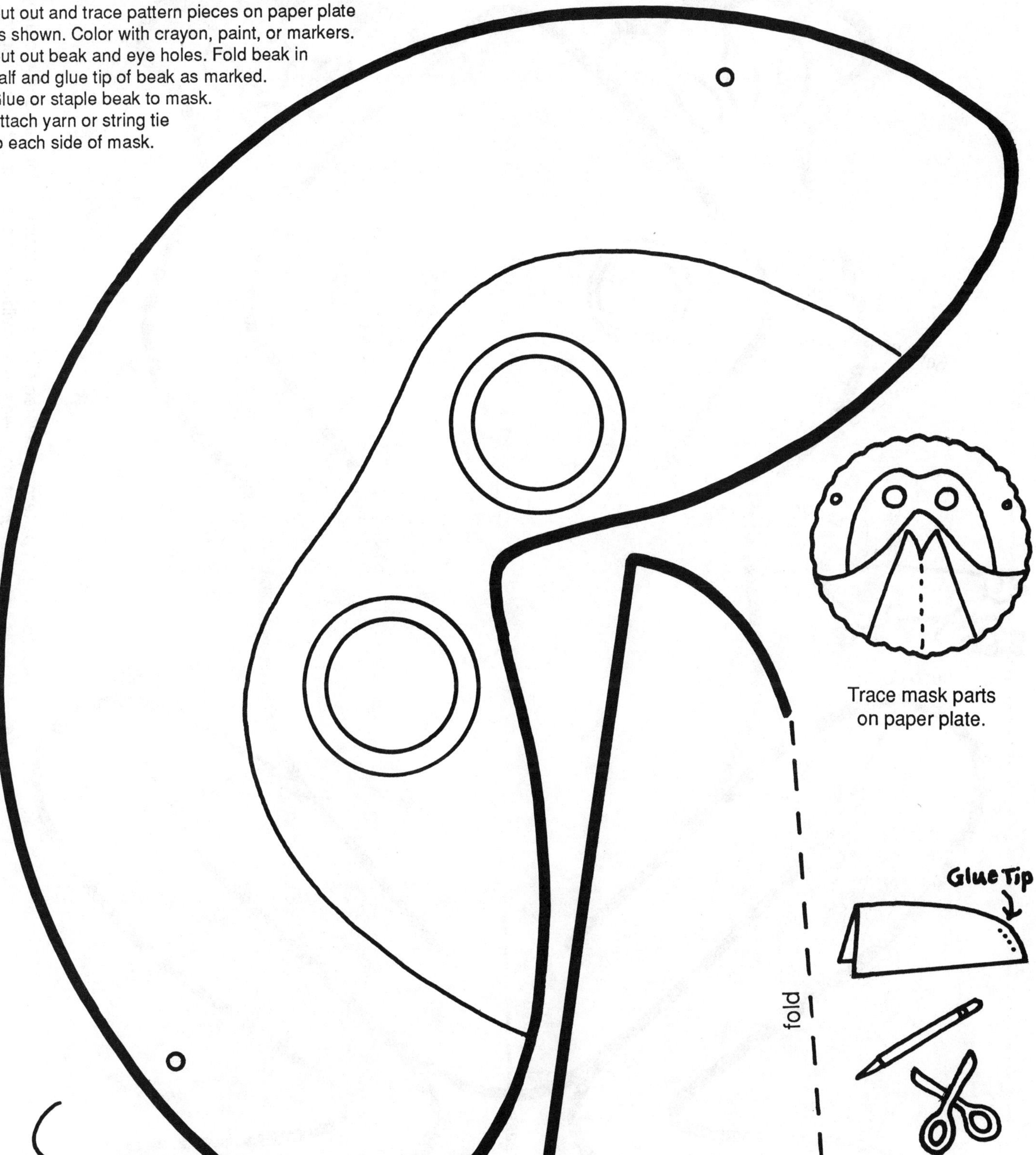

Trace mask parts on paper plate.

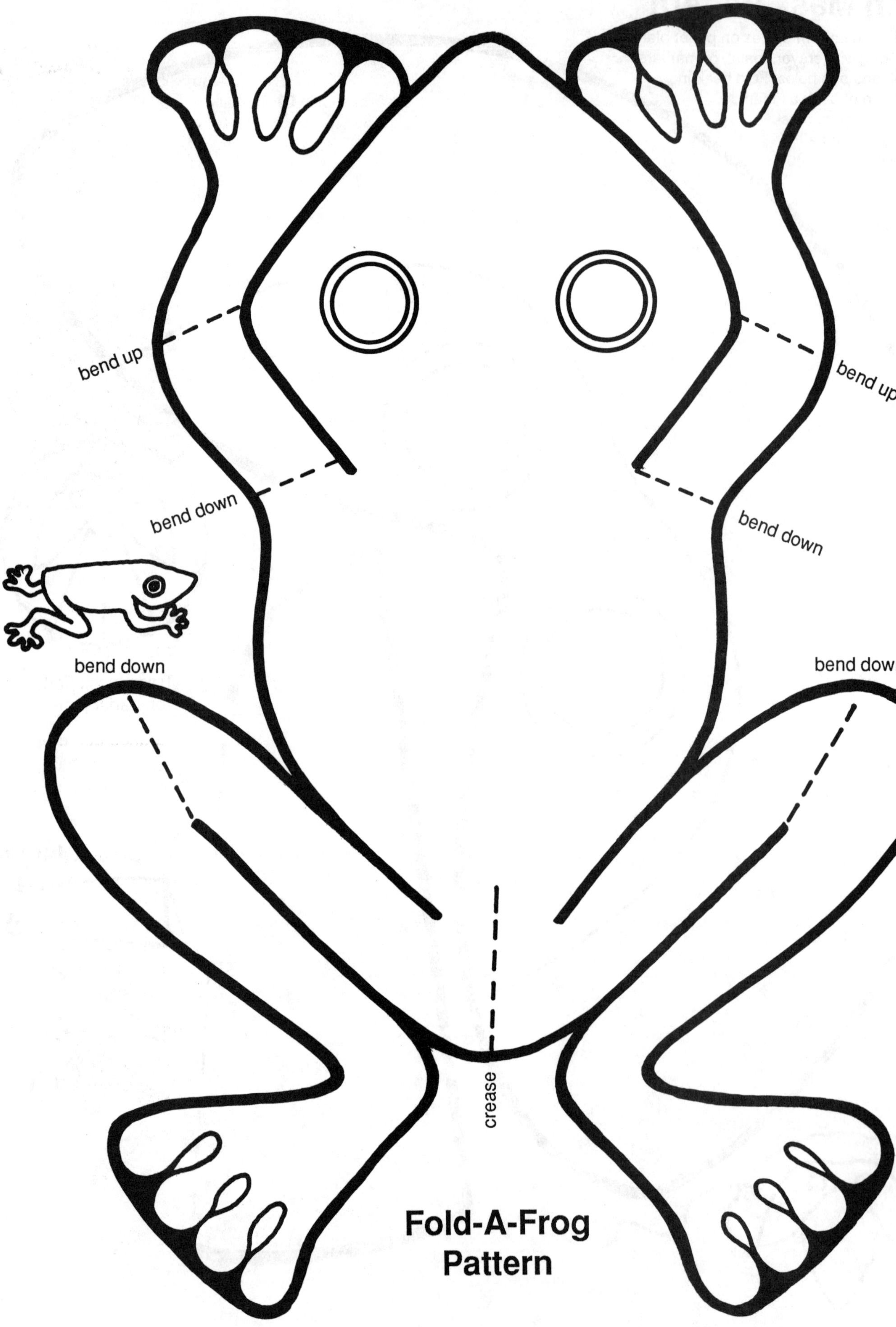

Fold-A-Frog Pattern

Reproduce frog pattern on colored construction paper. Color with chalk, crayons or paint. Rainforest frogs wear many vibrant colors. Cut out frog on solid lines; fold on dotted lines. Bend as marked to make frog sit.

PLANTS OF THE RAINFOREST

From top to bottom, the tropical rainforest is a world of lush green plants. More kinds of trees and plants grow here than in any other area in the world. Hot, humid conditions throughout the year support a diversity of plant life from shrubs, ferns, and colorful flowers to vines and giant towering trees. In this evergreen world, plants shed leaves continuously, a few at a time, as they grow rapidly in an ideal climate.

Although there is an amazing variety of plant life living in the rainforest, the soil is not very fertile. Most of the nutrients for plants are stored in the plants themselves or in a thin layer of decaying vegetation near the surface of the soil. Roots, found close to the surface, quickly absorb the nutrients. Since the root systems are so shallow, unusual roots called buttresses or stilt roots are needed for a strong base. Epiphytes, like the beautiful jungle orchids and bromeliads, use trees for support and get nutrients from dead leaves that fall from above. Lianas, woody vines that continually climb toward the sunlight, wind through the rainforest looking like a tangle of cobwebs. A complex system of layers, plants, ferns, shrubs, vines, and trees each have their own special niche in the tropical rainforest.

Ceiba

The leaf of the ceiba tree has a "drip tip." This kind of leaf ends in a sharp tip that hangs downward. Raindrops falling on the leaf quickly drain off and the water trickles down to the forest floor.

Cecropia

The cecropia is a short umbrella-shaped tree that grows very fast. It is found in sunny clearings in the understory of the rainforest. The leaves and seeds of the cecropia are eaten by birds, rodents, bats, and other animals. The cecropia's trunk and branches are hollow, making a good home for the azteca ants. The crecropia and the ants have formed a partnership. The tree is a home for the ants and the ants protect the tree from harmful insects and vines.

Orchid

The orchid is a beautiful flower that grows in the rainforest. It is an epiphyte and uses the branches and trunks of trees for support. Its brightly colored flower and powerful fragrance attract bees who drink the nectar and pollinate the orchid.

Tank Bromeliad

The tank bromeliad is an epiphyte that grows on the trunks and branches of trees. It has several wide leaves coming out from the center, surrounding a small pool of rainwater. The center forms a small garden, providing a home and a drink of water to many animals living in the canopy. Look for the plant patterns and directions for creating these plants from construction paper.

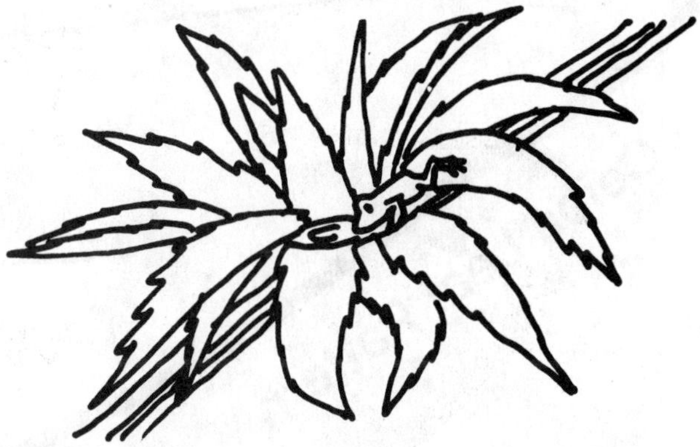

Kapok Tree

The kapok tree grows in the tropical rainforest. It has a short, thick trunk and many long branches. When the fruit of the tree is ripe, the seedpods are picked. The seedpods contain a light, soft cotton-like fiber which is used as a filling for mattresses, furniture, and life jackets.

Cacao Tree

The cacao tree has oblong, bright green leaves and is found in the understory of the rainforest. Large pods that look like melons grow from its trunk and branches. The pods contain many seeds or beans. Monkeys and small rodents break open the pods and scatter the seeds, planting other cacao trees. The seeds are used to make chocolate and cocoa.

Banana Plant

The banana plant looks like a tree but is actually a plant. The stalks of the leaves are similar to a "trunk" and as the leaves unroll, they look like large droopy feathers. Flowers on the plant become tiny green bananas that turn yellow and begin to curve upward as they grow. Bananas are picked green so that they will be ripe when they reach the market.

Rubber Tree

The hevea or rubber tree is a tall, straight, slender tree that grows in the rainforest. Latex containing rubber flows through tubes under the bark in the trunk of the tree. The latex is collected by cutting a groove in the bark and then catching the latex in a small cup. It must be taken to a factory to be made into rubber.

Palm

Many kinds of palms having different kinds of flowers, leaves, and fruits grow in the rainforest. Palms provide people with food, clothing, and building materials.

Fern

Ferns, which grow in many sizes and shapes, are plants without flowers. Some are so tiny they look like moss while others are as large as trees. The tree ferns have woody trunks with feathery crowns of large leaves. Smaller ferns that creep up tree trunks and grow high above the ground are called air plants.

Mushrooms

Mushrooms, fungi often shaped like small umbrellas, are everywhere in the rainforest. They can be found in many different shapes, sizes, and beautiful colors. Mushrooms grow on old trees and decaying plants and also in rich soil. When mushrooms grow on living plants they are called parasites.

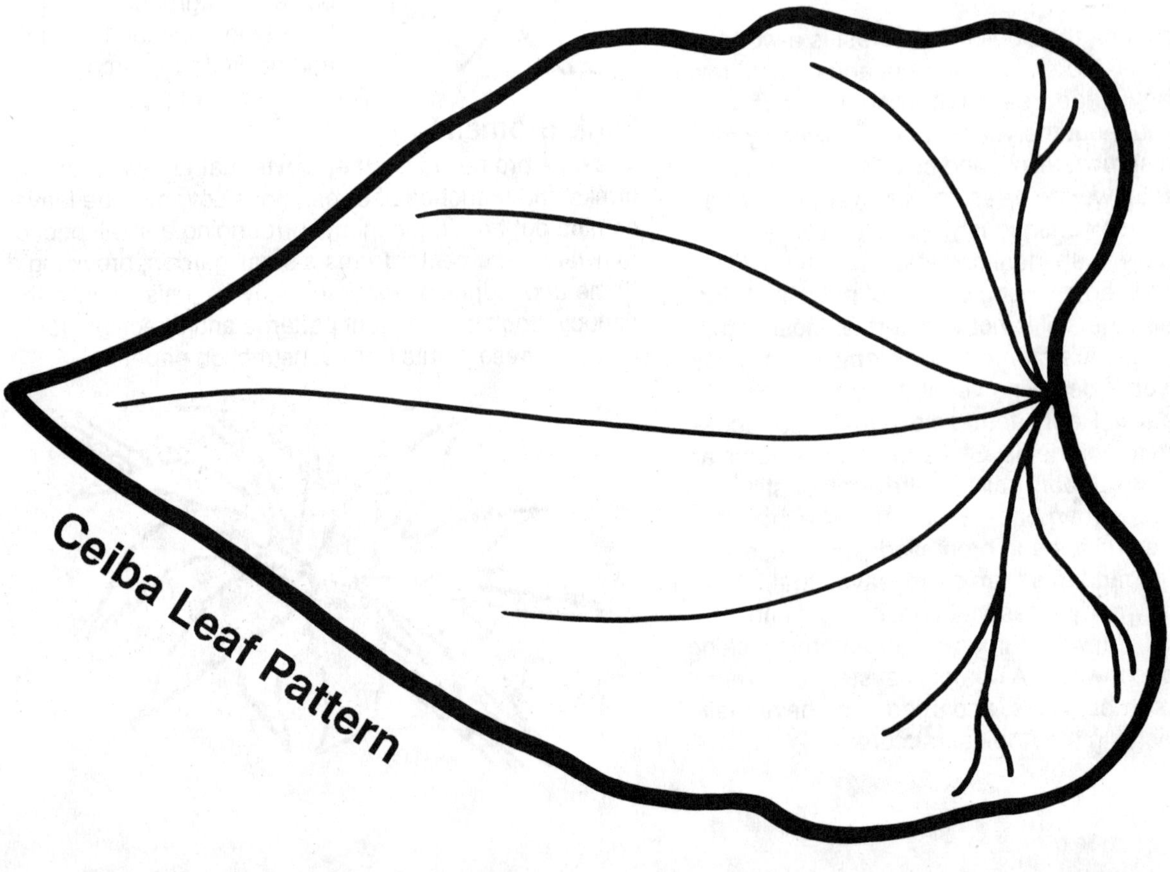

Rainforest Leaf Patterns

Enlarge these leaf patterns for your classroom rainforest trees.
Trace them on newspaper which has been painted green.

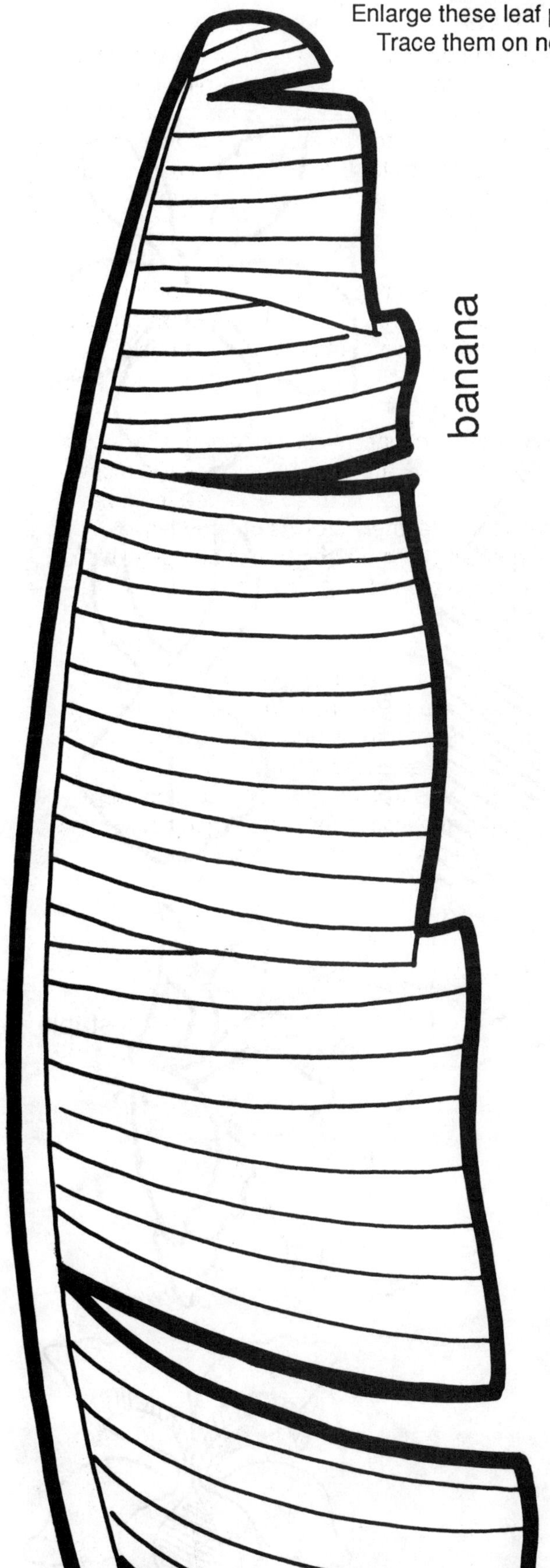

banana

rubber

cecropia

Orchid Pattern

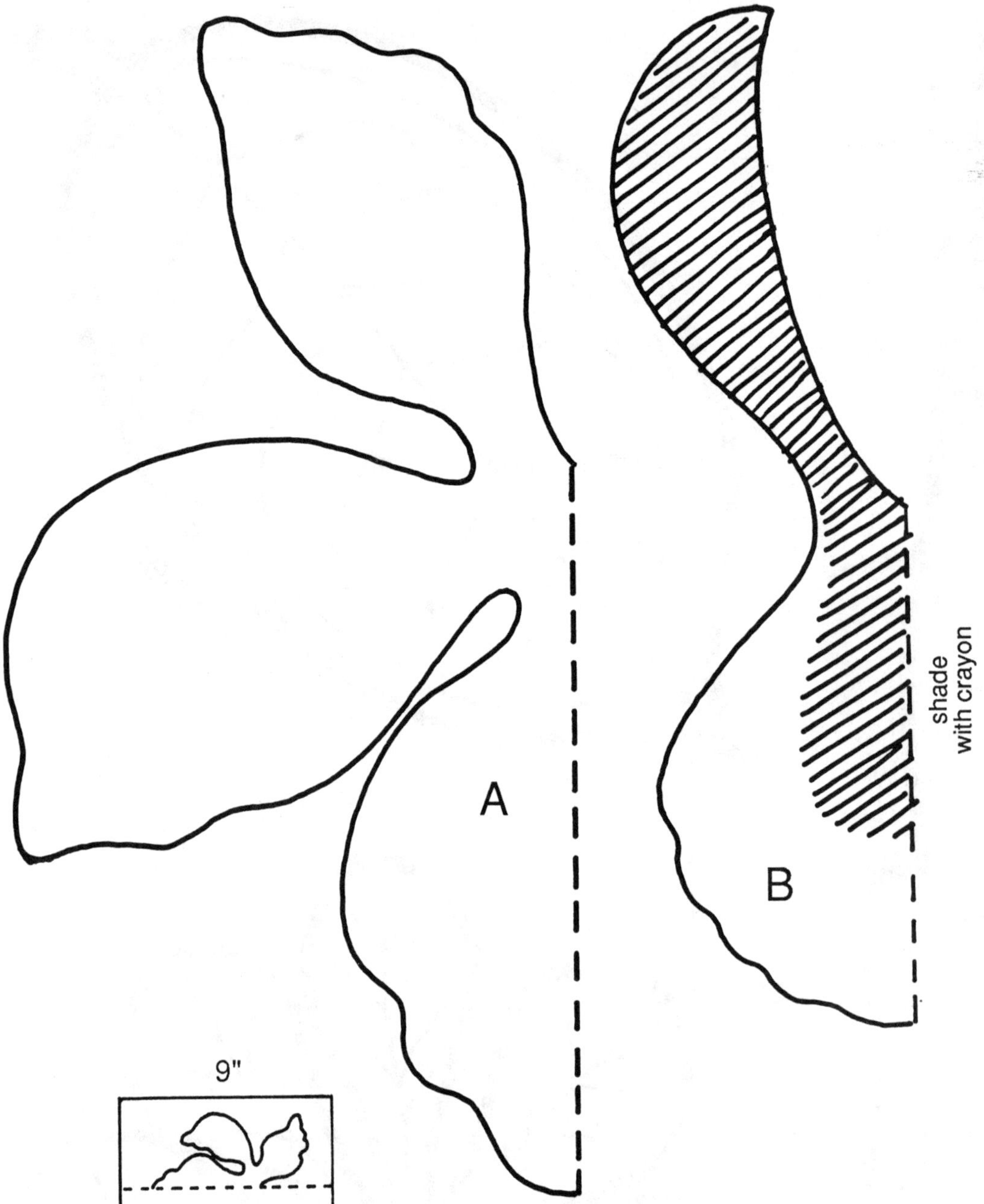

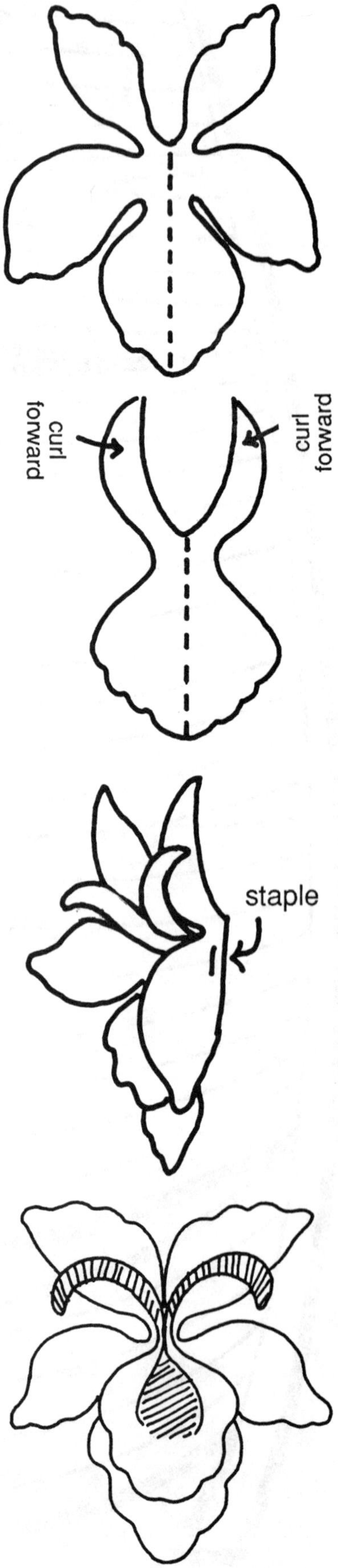

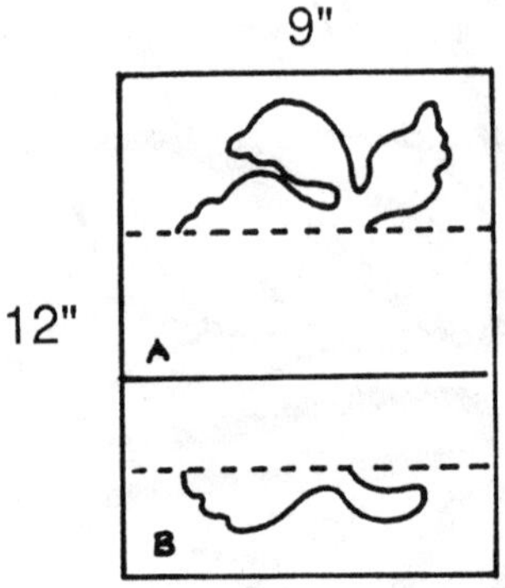

1. Trace parts A and B on colored construction paper, placing dotted lines on folds as shown in diagram. Cut out both pieces.
2. Choose a crayon a shade deeper than the paper color to color the shaded area on part B.
3. Place part B on top of part A. Crease and staple the sections together on center fold as shown in diagram at right.
4. Use your finger to curl the two “tails” on part B forward.
5. Attach the orchids to tree trunks and vines in your rainforest.

Bromeliad Pattern

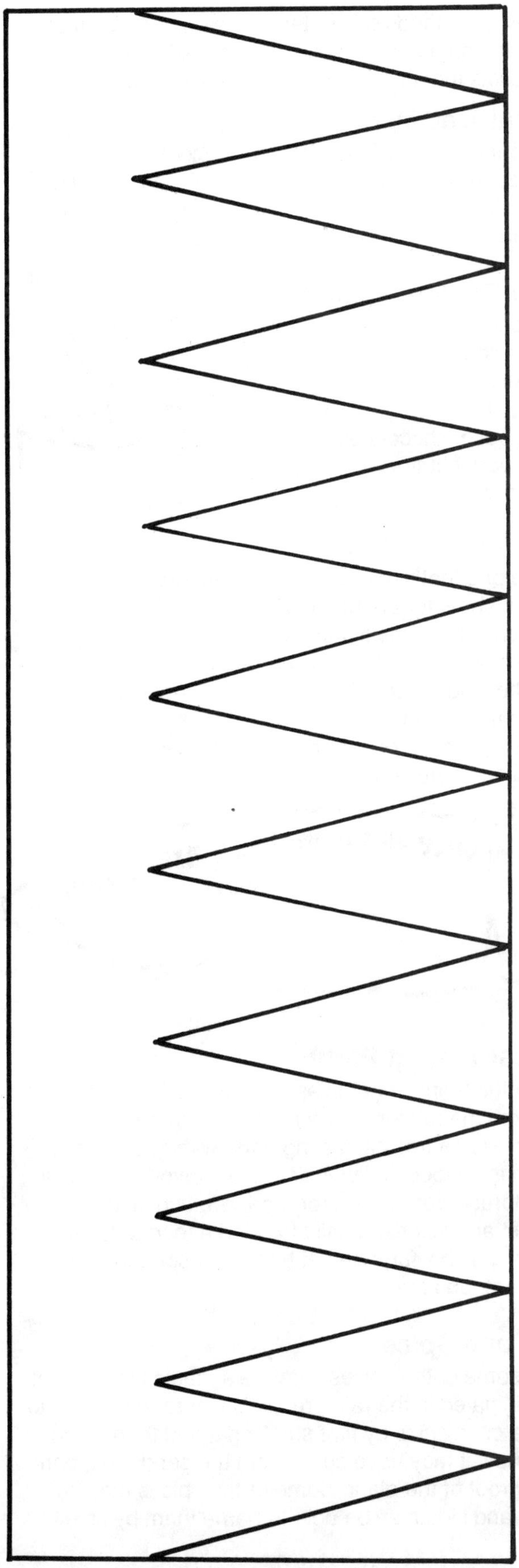

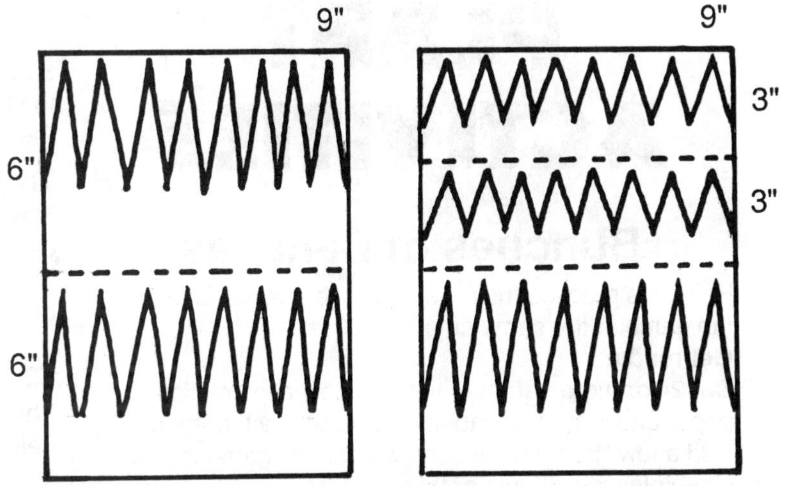

green paper   pink/red paper

1. Using pattern at left, trace and cut leaves across the 9-inch edge of 9"x12" construction paper. See diagram above.
2. Beginning with smallest pink leaves, wrap leaves around top of cup and glue in place. Follow with second smaller pink leaves, placing these leaves slightly below the first section. Glue in place. Follow with larger pink leaves.
3. Continue to layer the green leaves below the pink, in the same way.
4. When all leaves are in place, use your fingers to curl the leaves outward.
5. Reproduce a butterfly or beetle (below) for each flower. Color, cut out, and paste to a leaf on the bromeliad.
6. Optional: Put a little water inside the cup for the animal visitors.

PLANT ACTIVITIES

Bunches of Bananas

Help kids practice their reading vocabulary and play a fun game at the same time!

Get ready:

Cut 24 or more bananas out of yellow construction paper and write a vocabulary word on each banana. Add a few "freebies" with no words.This game is best when played with two or three children.

Play:

One child holds the bananas and drops them onto a playing surface. Some bananas will fall face up so that the children can see what the word will be while other bananas will hold mystery words. The first child picks a banana, reads the word, and uses it in a sentence. The turn continues until the child misses a word. The biggest bunch of bananas wins.

Leaf Limericks

Enlarge and trace the shape of one of the leaves on a sheet of construction paper. Use the shape of the leaf as a writing line, and encourage kids to write a limerick about the rainforest following the outline of the leaf.

Grow a Pineapple

The bromeliad is a member of the pineapple family. Grow a pineapple with its spiky leaves and compare it to a rainforest bromeliad! Here's how:

1. Choose a pineapple with a fresh, green top.
2. Cut off top leaving 1/3 inch of the fruit attached and allow top to dry overnight.
3. In the morning scrape away the fruit that is still soft and moist, leaving center untouched.
4. Place top in pot containing moist soil and a layer of pebbles on the bottom.
5. Cover top with a large plastic bag and place in a warm, sunny spot.
6. Remove bag when new leaves appear in center.

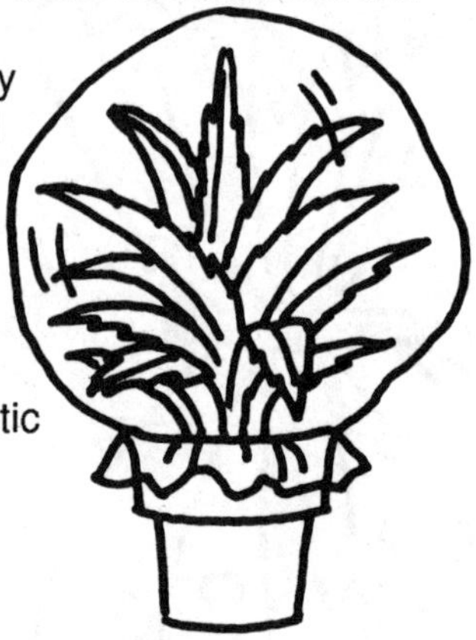

Tropical Treats

So many good foods originated in the rainforest. Treat the kids to some special snacks to remind them of all the products that come from the rainforest.

Tropical Trail Mix

Make your own tropical trail mix by blending Brazil nuts, cashews, shredded coconut, macadamia nuts, peanuts, banana chips, and chocolate chips. An easy end-of-the-day treat!

Choco-Banana Snacks

Three foods that grow in the rainforest equal one delicious snack!

You'll need:

6 large bananas
12-oz. pkg. chocolate chips
1 c. peanut butter
toothpicks

Directions:

1. Slice bananas into 1-inch pieces.
2. Place one toothpick in each slice and freeze on a cookie sheet for about 1 hour.
3. Melt chocolate chips and peanut butter together in a double boiler or a microwave.
4. Dip the cold banana slices into the chocolate/peanut butter mixture to cover.
5. Place on waxed paper until firm. Store in plastic container in freezer.

Tropical Tasting Party

Many of the fruits, vegetables, nuts and other foods that come from the rainforest are not familiar foods to children. Plan a tropical tasting party with some of the more unusual foods as well as the old favorites. Check the rainforest products list for foods we find in the rainforest and ask each child to bring a food to taste. The kids may be surprised at how tasty some of those unfamiliar foods are!

Sugar and Spice

Collect some of the spices—nature's magic flavor—that have originated in the rainforests. Encourage the kids to examine each spice by first smelling it and then trying to determine if it may have come from the seed, fruit, bark, stem, or root of the plant. Some of the spices may be familiar, and kids may be able to name them by smell.

Spicey Cashew Cookies

Here's an easy cookie recipe using spices found in the rainforest... and the cashews can be found there too!

Ingredients:

1/2 c. shortening (half butter and half shortening)
1-1/4 c. brown sugar (firmly packed)
1 egg
1-3/4 c. flour
2 t. baking powder
1/2 t. each salt, ginger, cinnamon, cloves, & nutmeg
1/3 cup chopped cashews

Directions:

Mix shortening, sugar, and egg in large mixing bowl. Measure dry ingredients and stir into shortening mixture. Stir in chopped cashews. Roll dough in 1-inch balls and place on greased cookie sheet. Flatten slightly and bake at 375° for 10 to 12 minutes. Makes 4 to 5 dozen cookies.

Tapioca Cream Pudding

Tapioca is a food made by heating the starch from the root of the manioc, a plant found in the rainforest. Kids may have already tried tapioca pudding, but if they haven't, a small taste of tapioca pudding will be a hit!

Ingredients:

1 egg slightly beaten
1/3 c. sugar
3 T. quick-cooking tapioca
1/8 teaspoon salt
2-1/2 c. milk
1 t. vanilla

Directions:

Mix egg, sugar, tapioca, salt, and milk in a pan. Let stand for 5 minutes. Cook over medium heat, stirring constantly until mixture comes to a full boil. Add vanilla and remove from heat. Cool. Fold in sliced bananas and flaked coconut for an added surprise from the tropics.

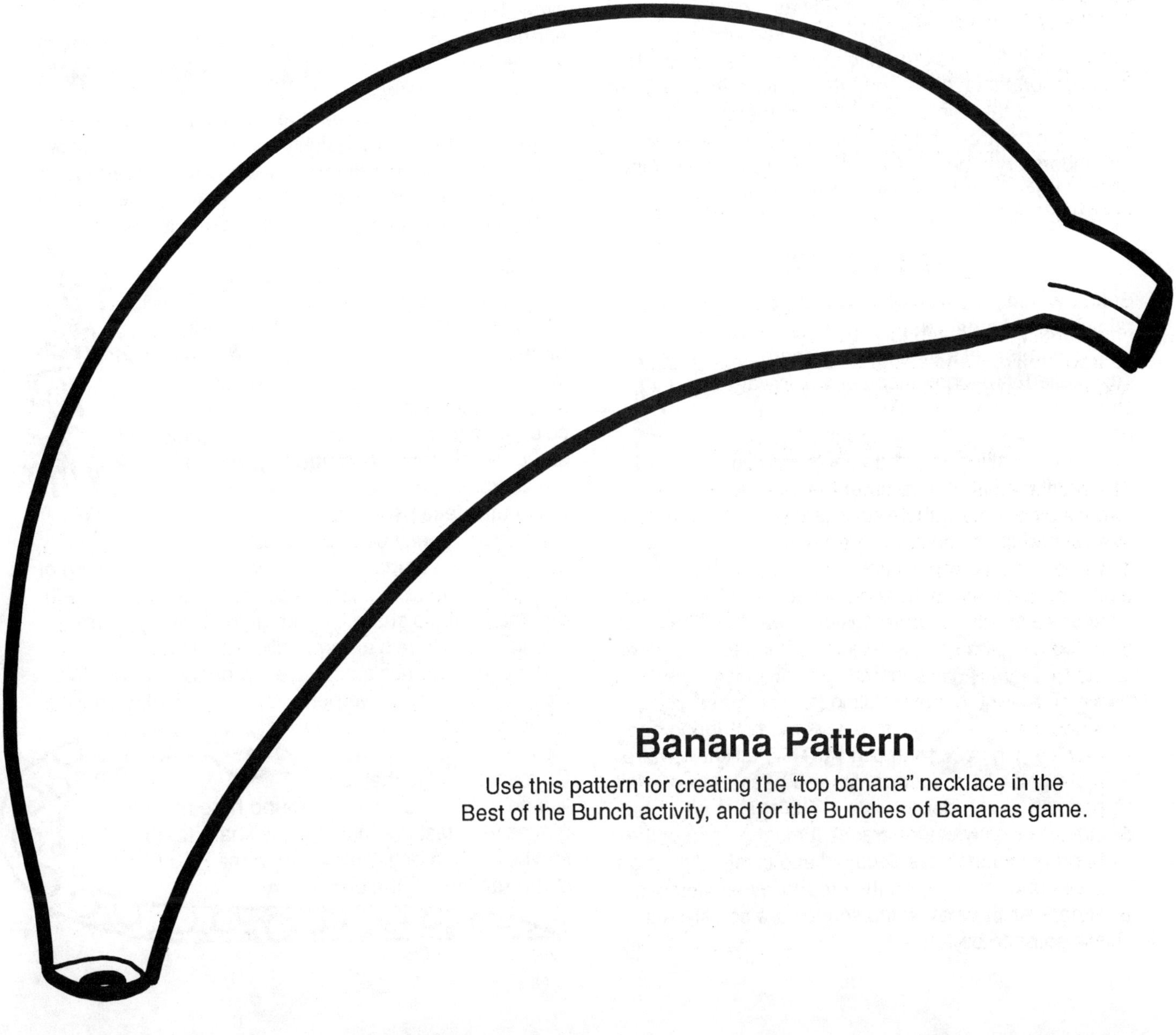

Banana Pattern

Use this pattern for creating the "top banana" necklace in the Best of the Bunch activity, and for the Bunches of Bananas game.

TAKE A WALK ON THE WILD SIDE!

Invite kids on an imaginary walk through a tropical rainforest. Encourage them to visualize and feel the sights and sounds deep within this jungle paradise. Don the safari hats and grab the binoculars because you never know what you may see in this mysterious place. Don't forget your official rainforest observer badges and you're ready to go.

Teacher Tips

Ask each child to color and glue together the reproducible layers of the rainforest to use as a guide on your walk. Critter Cards will help the kids see what the animals look like. Ask them to place the cards next to the appropriate layer as you talk. Remind students that the layers of the rainforest blend together and animals that live in the trees often live in both the canopy and the understory. Then pull the shades, play a recording of rainforest sounds, add your own ideas to the narrative, and "Take A Walk On the Wild Side."

Narrative

Before we begin our exciting walk through a tropical rainforest, we must cut through these thick shrubs and tangled vines. Let's use this very sharp knife called a machete and cut a pathway so that we can walk in. There we are! It's beautiful... and dark...and green in here. The air feels still, cool, and very damp. Do you smell the rich earthy smell? Look up! See those tall trees, the roof of green leaves, and the beautifully colored flowers way up there. It covers us like an umbrella. We can't even see the sun. No wonder it's so dark in here. Listen! Hear the sounds of the insects buzzing and the birds chirping, screeching, and calling to each other. The monkeys are chattering and howling. They all know we're here. Do you hear that waterfall trickling into a little stream off in the distance? What was that crash? It must be one of the large branches that has decayed and is falling through the trees and crashing on the ground. What else can you hear? All the sights and sounds are so different. This is going to be fun!

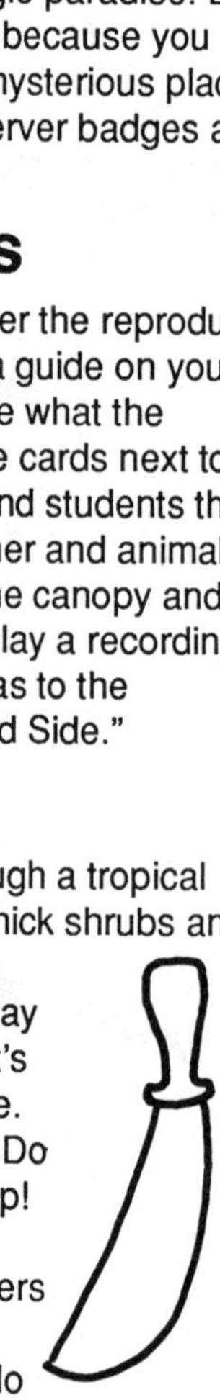

The Forest Floor

As we walk along the forest floor, we can feel the damp moss and the decaying leaves and branches under our feet. It feels just like a soft carpet. There is no wind and the leaves high above us keep out most of the sunlight. It's dark, even in the daytime. Ferns, gingers, and other small plants are growing on the forest floor. The soil looks rich because there are so many beautiful, green plants growing all around us. But the rainforest soil is not very fertile. All the rain washes the soil's nutrients away. Look carefully! Do you see the termites, earthworms, millipedes, and beetles? These insects have a very special job to do. They eat the decaying plants and animals. Nutrients are quickly recycled into the shallow root systems of the rainforest trees to make them grow green and lush. Frogs and toads are everywhere. Don't step on them. Look at that... a parade of leaves! No, it isn't a parade of leaves. Those are the leafcutter ants bringing leaves to their underground nest. They grow fungus in their nest and that's what they eat. My goodness, there are a lot of insects living here. That wood turtle moves so slowly, but watch out for those famous marching army ants. Some colonies march in long lines with as many as 20 million ants. Their strong jaws eat all the scorpions, millipedes, and other bugs in their path...even some of the small animals! If we stand quietly behind this bush we may be able to see some of the animals that look for food on the floor of the rainforest. Poisonous snakes like the fer-de-lance with its sharp fangs may be looking for frogs and lizards. There's an armadillo with its sharp claws looking for a termite's nest. He's probably hungry. We're close to the river so we better be on the lookout for that giant snake, the anaconda. He may live nearby. The Caimen, a reptile that looks like an alligator, also lives around here and he moves very fast and has awfully sharp teeth. Maybe we had better move up to the next layer of the rainforest...the understory.

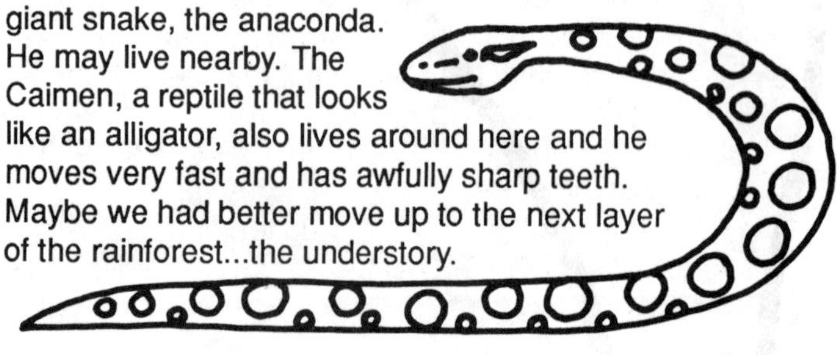

The Understory

Now, look up from the rainforest floor to see the next layer of the rainforest. It is called the understory. There isn't much light here either because the sun's light has a hard time getting through all the thick leaves up above. The shrubs, palms, and young trees growing around us like growing in shade. Someday some of these trees may be part of the higher rainforest layers. Look at the large leaves on the trees. These large leaves help the trees absorb as much sunlight as possible in the shadowy understory. Oh, there's an opening over there in the trees...a dying tree must have fallen to the ground. The sunlight can shine through now to the layers below. The sun will help the plants grow quickly. It won't be long before new trees will fill up this opening.

The understory looks like many tree trunks and a tangle of branches and vines. Animals that live here in the shadows must be clever in order to find food and safe shelter. They have learned to cling, leap, swing, and even fly from branch to branch. Spider monkeys hang from the branches by their tails and pick fruit and leaves to eat. That tamandua anteater has his tail wrapped around a branch so he won't fall off as he looks for termites to eat. The red-eyed tree frogs have special pads on their toes to help them cling to the trees. Instead of leaping, these frogs creep gently along the branches. The flying squirrel will amaze you as it leaps from one tree and glides to another. Flaps of skin stretched between its front and back legs are like a parachute. Look closely— you might even spot flying frogs, flying lizards, and flying snakes in the understory. That scary-looking iguana looks like it belongs in a spooky movie along with that hairy tarantula. The anole lizard on that tree branch has long toes and sticky pads which make it a good climber. Watch out for the big cats like the jaguar and ocelot that hide in the trees, waiting to catch small animals. Snakes like the bright orange tree boa and the false coral snake sleep during the day so that they can hunt at night. Most of the insects living in the rainforest live here in the understory. Many animals, like the tropical bats, eat these insects. Did you know that one bat can eat as many as 3,000 insects in just one night? Other bats like to eat the nectar from the beautiful flowers. Without knowing it, these bats get covered with pollen. As they fly from flower to flower, they pollinate other plants. Some bats eat tropical fruits. They crush the fruit with their strong teeth and spread the seeds throughout the rainforest. Bats are important to the rainforest.

The Canopy

Look up even higher. Do you see something that looks like a giant roof made of trees and vines? That's the canopy. The trees can grow as tall as a 17-story building! A tree this big needs help standing up in the soil of the rainforest. Broad fans of roots called buttresses support the tree. The canopy is like a huge umbrella over the rainforest. It keeps the rain and sunlight from reaching the understory and the forest floor. The treetops are flat and the leaves twist and turn and help catch the rain. If you look closely, you will notice that the leaves have a pointed shape. Those are called "drip tips." The rain drips right off the tips of these leaves. As the rainwater runs off, it trickles down the trunks of the trees to the forest floor.

The canopy is like a gigantic wildlife park. You can find plants and animals in every nook and cranny. Most of the rainforest plants and animals live somewhere here in the canopy. You might see spider monkeys swinging among the branches. There are opossums and two-toed sloths looking for food. Hold your ears. Noisy howler monkeys are dangling from the trees, munching on fruit. Thousands of birds live in the canopy. Look at the colorful parrots, tiny hummingbirds, the paradise tanager, and big-billed toucans. Do you hear the screeching macaws? What do you think of that interesting nest the oropendola is making? There are bright butterflies and camouflaged moths. The flowers up here are beautiful. Those orchids are some of the prettiest flowers and they grow right here in the canopy. The other plant growing on the trunk of that tree is called a bromeliad. Its leaves form a little bowl to catch rainwater. The bowl makes a nice home for tropical frogs, salamanders, birds, and insects. Do you think we've reached the top of the rainforest? Not yet! There's still one more layer— the emergent layer!

Emergent Layer

As we look even higher, we see that the trees in the canopy were tall, but the trees in the emergent layer are the giants of the rainforest. They're skyscrapers! There are only a few of these giant trees. The tops of these trees are umbrella-shaped and their trunks are long and thin. The leaves are thick and waxy so they can hold water. Nothing keeps the hot temperatures and the strong winds from these leaves. You may spot some birds and butterflies living here. The huge harpy eagle stands watch high above the rainforest. Watch as it swoops down under the crowns of the trees in the canopy and and tries to grab that sloth clinging to a branch. Oops! Missed it!

Well, we've finally reached the top. The rainforest has been a wonderful place to visit and we learned so much about the plants and animals that make their home here. But, I guess its time to go home now. I'm sure glad we don't have to climb down!

Safari Hat Pattern

Reproduce this safari hat on brown paper. Cut out. Cut a 2-inch strip of paper to fit around child's head. Staple the head band to the back of the hat pattern.

Create binoculars for your safari outing by taping together two cardboard tubes cut from paper towel rolls. Add a length of yarn or string for wearing them around the neck.

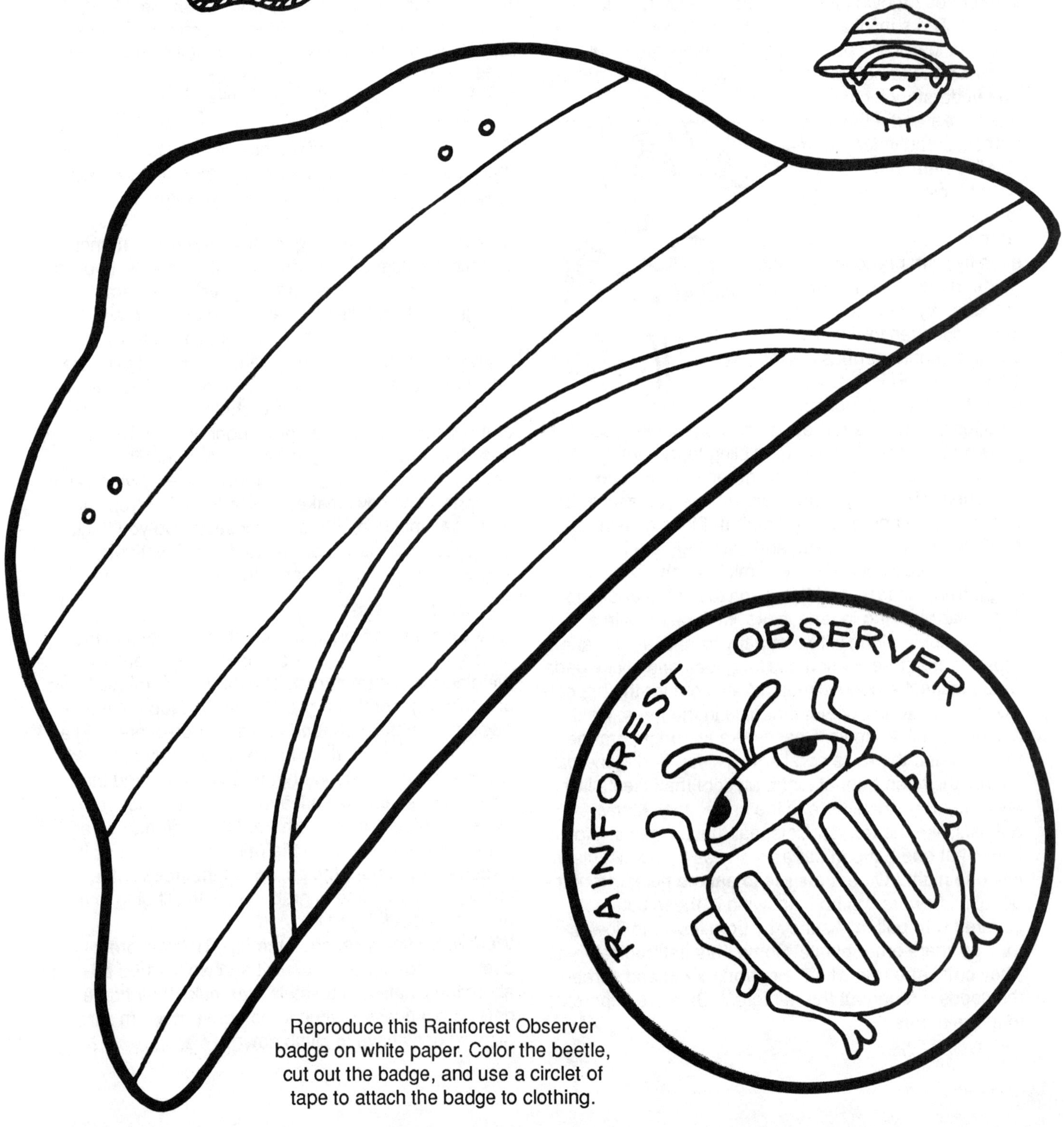

Reproduce this Rainforest Observer badge on white paper. Color the beetle, cut out the badge, and use a circlet of tape to attach the badge to clothing.

Instant Vocabulary

Post these rainforest words on a chart in a prominent place in the classroom. Encourage children to use the words in their creative writing, poetry, and other rainforest projects. No one will need to ask for the spelling of a word and it will help to review important terms.

biodiversity · bromeliad
buttress · canopy · conservation
deforestation · drip tips
emergent · endangered species
epiphyte · equator · extinct
forest floor · liana · parasite
tropical rainforest
understory

Rainforest Glossary

Children may use these and other words to make their own rainforest glossary. Assign one word each day. After carefully writing the word and its definition, ask the kids to write the word in a sentence and draw a picture to illustrate the word. Younger children can make a glossary with just the word and a picture. Class rainforest glossaries may be created by assigning one word to each child to define and illustrate. Bind the pages together, add a cover, and keep it as an easy reference with your rainforest display.

DRIP TIPS - Leaves that come to a point allowing rain water to drip off.

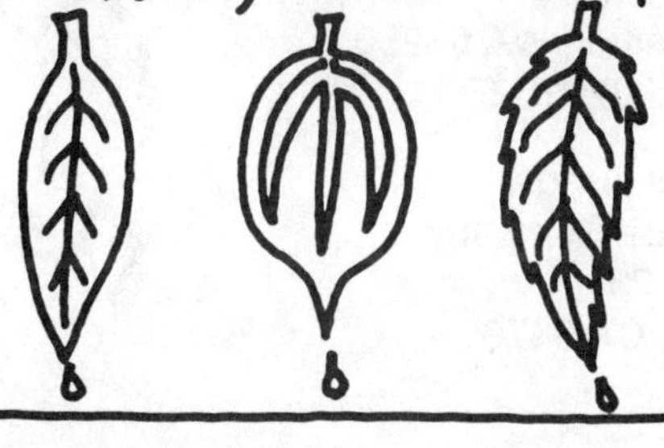

biodiversity— many different kinds of life.

bromeliad— a tropical plant, a member of the pineapple family, that grows on the branches or trunks of trees.

buttress— a fan shaped bottom on some of the tall rainforest trees that helps hold the tree upright.

canopy— a thick, overhead layer of the forest made by the tops of tall trees and vines.

conservation— a careful preservation and protection of something.

deforestation— the process of stripping an area of trees and other vegetation.

drip tips— leaves that come to a point allowing rainwater to drip off.

emergent— a layer of the forest where some trees grow taller than the trees around it.

endangered species— an animal or plant that is threatened with extinction.

epiphyte— a plant that grows on another plant, but does not harm it.

equator— the imaginary line around the earth halfway between the North and South Poles.

extinct— no longer living.

forest floor— the bottom layer of the rainforest.

liana— a woody vine that is rooted in the soil and grows up tree trunks.

parasite— a plant or animal that grows and feeds on another.

tropical rainforest— an evergreen forest found in an area around the equator. There is much rainfall and the climate is warm and humid year round. Sometimes called a jungle.

understory— the layer of the forest below the canopy where small trees, shrubs, and herbs grow.

RAINFOREST RESOURCES

Poetry

Prelutsky, Jack. "Toucan Two"
Toucans Two and Other Poems (Macmillan, 1970)

Silverstein, Shel. "The Toucan"
Where the Sidewalk Ends (Harper & Row, 1974)

Storybooks

Baker, Jeannie. ***Where the Forest Meets the Sea***
(Greenwillow Books, 1987)
A young boy visits a forest near the sea. He pretends it is long ago as he walks among the ancient trees of an Australian tropical rainforest. He wonders how much longer the forest will remain.

Catchpole, Dr. Clive. ***The Living World: Jungles***
(Dial Books, 1984)
Colorful illustrations tell about interrelationships and adaptations necessary for survival in the world's rainforests.

Catterwell, Thelma. ***Aldita and the Forest***
(Houghton Mifflin, 1989)
Newborn butterfly Aldita, left alone by her own kind, finds herself in an Australian forest. She learns about "the plan" when she is befriended by other creatures. A colorful picture book.

Cherry, Lynne. ***The Great Kapok Tree***
(Harcourt Brace Jovanovich, 1990)
When a man begins cutting down one of the rainforest's mighty trees, he becomes tired and lies down to rest. While sleeping, the animals living in the tree whisper in his ear. They tell him why he should not destroy their home. The story and illustrations provide a close-up look at the beauty of the Amazon rainforest and its inhabitants. It's a great starter for discussion about the importance of the rainforests and the effect destruction of it will have on its inhabitants.

Cobb, Vicki. ***This Place Is Wet***
(Walker and Company, 1989)
Focuses on the land, ecology, people and animals of the Amazon rainforest in Brazil, presenting it as an example of a place where there is so much water that some houses need to be built on stilts.

Cowcher, Helen. ***Rain Forest***
(Farrar, Straus and Giroux, 1988)
One day a large machine is heard in the rainforest and the animals scurry from their homes. When the machine crashes and disappears into a large hole, the animals return, but they are uncertain how long they will be able to remain. Splashes of color give the reader the feeling of a tropical rainforest and readers realize that there is more to a rainforest than just trees. The book, with its striking illustrations, will help introduce rainforest animals to your class.

Dorros, Arthur. ***Rain Forest Secrets***
(Scholastic Inc., 1990)
A close-up look at the amazing variety of plants and animals that make their home in the different layers of the rainforest—more kinds of plants and animals than anywhere else on earth. A wonderful introduction to the ecosystem of the rainforest and its fragility.

Facklam, Margery. ***And Then There Was One***
(Little, Brown & Co., 1990)
A picture book with an important message, this book talks about the mysteries of extinction. It addresses the issues of taking over animal habitats, causing species to become extinct.

George, Jean Craighead. ***One Day in the Tropical Rain Forest*** (Harper Collins, 1990)
The future of the rainforest of the macaw depends on a scientist and a young Indian boy as they search for a nameless butterfly during one day in the rainforest.

Pittaway, Margaret. ***The Rainforest Children***
(Oxford University Press, 1980)
The rainforest children travel from their home in a Queensland rainforest to a different habitat, a land of sea and sand. The story tells about the contrasting habitats.

Recordings

"Jungle" Nature Recordings Vol. V
P.O. Box 2749
Friday Harbor, WA 98250
Phone (800) 228-5711

"Tropical Jungle"
The Nature Company
P.O. Box 2310
Berkeley, CA 94702

"Sounds of a Tropical Rainforest in America"
Carolina Biological Supply Company
2700 York Road, Burlington, NC 27215

Videos

3-2-1 Contact — You Can't Grow Home Again is an Emmy award-winning video of the Costa Rican rainforest. One-hour VCR tape. Write: The Video Project, 5332 College Avenue, Suite 101, Oakland CA 94618 or phone (415) 655-9050.

Vanishing Rain Forests is a 6-minute video rap with poster and teacher's guide for grades 2-6. Write: World Wildlife Fund, P.O. Box 4866, Hampden Post Office, Baltimore, MD 21211 or phone (301) 338-6951.

Adopt A Rainforest

For just $30, your class can purchase an acre of rainforest and receive an honorary land deed. Known as the Rio Bravo Conservation Area, 100% of your money goes into a fund to buy land in northwestern Belize. Contact: Nature Conservancy, 1815 North Lynn Street, Arlington, VA 22209.

Classroom Materials

Rainforest: Tropical Treasures (Naturescope, Volume 16 Order No. 75044) is a comprehensive 68-page activity book for teachers of grades K-8. Write: National Wildlife Federation, 1400 16th Street NW, Washington, DC 20036 or phone 1-800-432-6564.

Rainforests: Kids for Conservation is a 13-page teacher guide which includes activities for grades K-12. Write: Marine World Africa USA, Marine World Foundation, Marine World Parkway, Vallejo, CA 94589.

Rainforest Action Guide is an 8-page guide to rainforest activism. It answers questions and provides resources. A poster, "Save the Rainforest," is also offered. Write: Rainforest Action Network, 301 Broadway, Suite A, San Francisco, CA 94133.

Rainforest Curriculum Packet (K-8) includes activities, posters, and resources on the rainforests. Write: Rainforest Alliance, 270 Lafayette Street, Suite 512, New York, NY 10012.

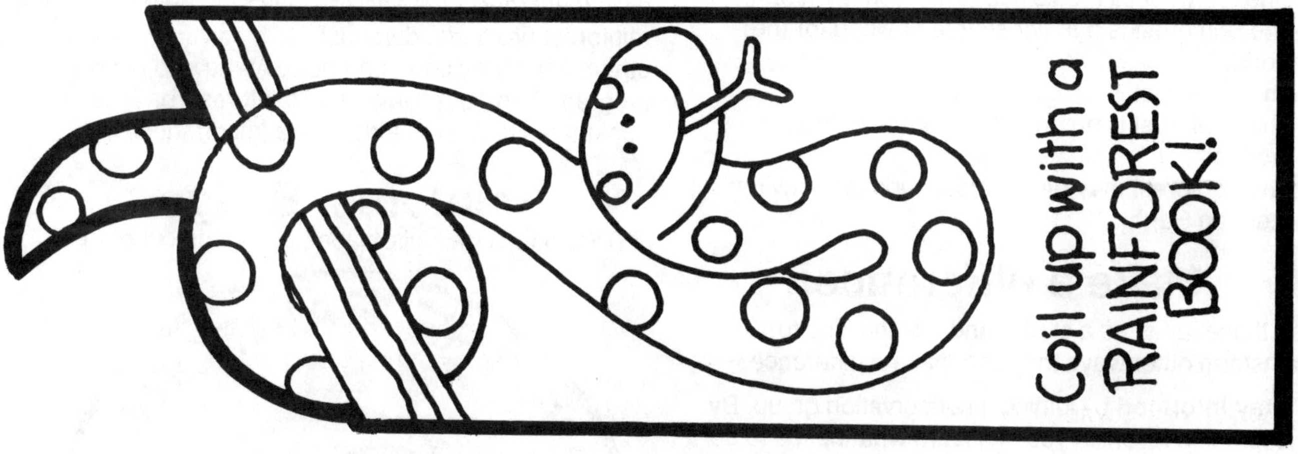

Rainforest Bookmarks

IT'S NOT EASY STAYING GREEN

Saving the World's Rainforests...

Rainforests have been around for about 100 million years but because of the rapid deforestation in recent years, our rainforests are now in danger. Loss of trees due to logging, farming, ranching, and new development is a real problem. Deforestation contributes to global warming; it upsets the earth's very delicate ecosystem and we are all affected. John Muir once said, "When we try to pick out one thing by itself, we find it hitched to everything else in the universe." It's not easy staying green...the rainforests need our help.

What's so special about our rainforests?

- The rainforest is home to half the plant and animal species on Earth. Many of those plants and animals have not yet been discovered. Many are becoming extinct.
- 40% of the Earth's oxygen comes from the rainforest.
- The rainforest is home to important medicinal plants. One fourth of all medicines come from plants.
- The rainforest is a major source of wood for the world.
- The rainforest is home to old cultures.
- The rainforest is an important source of food products.
- The rainforest may be the most important environment on Earth.

Make a difference!

Use these ideas as a starter and ask the kids to brainstorm other ways they can make a difference.

- **Stay Informed** by joining a conservation group. By becoming involved you can learn what needs to be done and how you can help. Read and learn about a specific animal that lives in the rainforest.
- **Practice Conservation** by becoming an energy saver. Turn off the lights, shut off running water faucets, use recycled paper, turn down the heat, use less hot water, and walk instead of riding. Become a recycler by starting a recycling center for your family or your school. Collect discarded newspapers, aluminum, glass, and plastic.
- **Educate Others** by sharing your information with others to let them know about the rainforest. Spread the word by writing letters to newspapers or making posters. Plan a Rainforest Awareness Day for kids at your school.

After brainstorming and listing the many ways we can make a difference, ask each student to copy and then illustrate one of the ideas on a 12"x18" sheet of paper. Create a cover and bind all of the ideas and illustrations into a book...***50 Ways to Help Save the Rainforest.***

Rainforest Awareness Day

Make your Rainforest Awareness Day a day that is planned and implemented by the kids. Kids have wonderful ideas and, with a little brainstorming, can make it a worthwhile and rewarding day. A few suggestions and a little direction from adults may be helpful. Begin by advertising your Rainforest Awareness Day with posters hung in the halls. Everyone can get into the act with this one. Provide lots of paper, crayons, markers, paint, and a few slogans... "Save Our Rainforests," "Make a Difference," "Keep it Green." Then turn the kids loose. Everyone will soon be wondering what all this is about.

Invite other classes to visit your classroom rainforest. Give tours, describe different rainforest animals, display rainforest products, demonstrate biodiversity, and tell others what they can do to help. At the end of your program, hand out "Save the Rainforest" badges and bookmarks to remind kids of this important day.

Rainforest Badge

(Reproduce on white paper, color, and cut out.)

Monkey Pattern

Reproduce monkey parts on brown or gray paper. Cut out parts and use brass paper fasteners to connect limbs & tail to body.

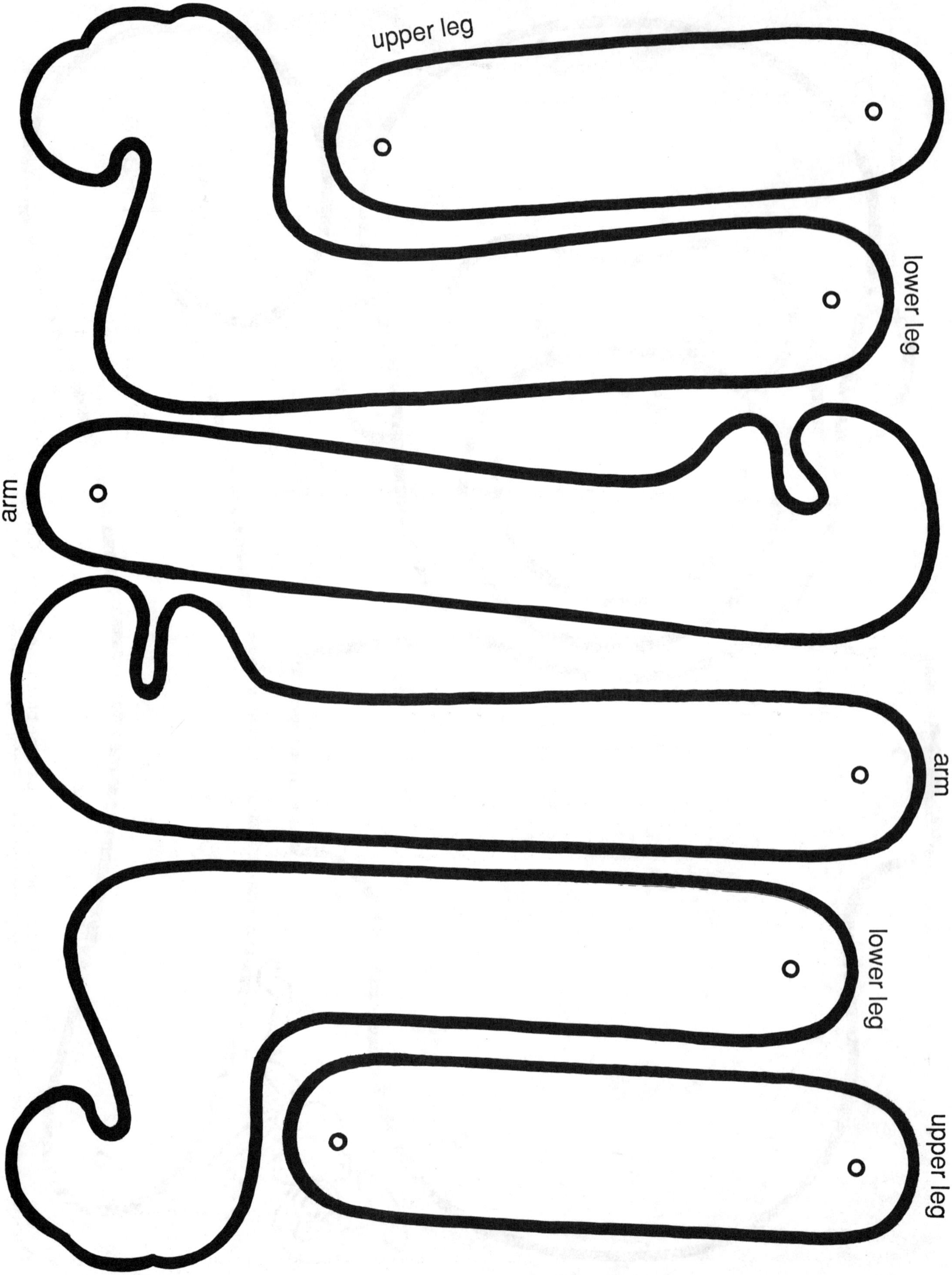
upper leg
lower leg
arm
arm
lower leg
upper leg

Monkey T-Shirt Pattern

Reproduce T-shirt on colored construction paper. Write a rainforest slogan on the shirt. Paste shirt on monkey. Some ideas for T-shirt slogans: "Rescue the Rainforest," "Keep It Green," "Save My Home."

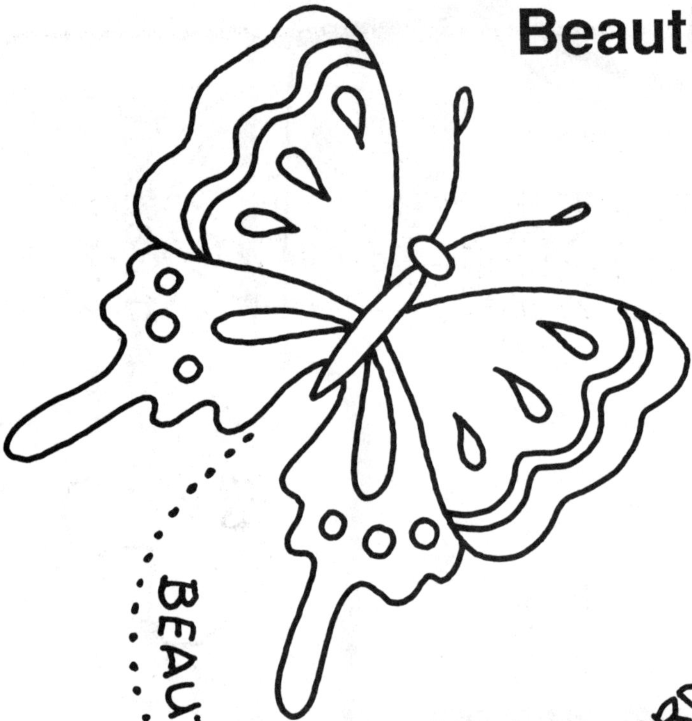

Beautiful Butterfly Award

presented to

____
(name)

____
(date)

BEAUTIFUL BUTTERFLY AWARD for beautiful handwriting!

____
(signature)

FINE FROG AWARD

presented to

____
(name)

for being a **SUPER** helper!

____
(date)

____
(signature)

FRIEND of the ENVIRONMENT PLEDGE

I promise to be a friend to the environment.
I will respect nature.
I will not litter.
I will be a recycler.
I will conserve energy.
I will encourage others to be
a friend to the environment.
I will make a difference.

____

signature

RESCUE the **RAINFOREST**

Toucans

This is a toucan.
It is a rainforest bird.
It has a big beak.
It has bright feathers.

Color this big bird.
Draw it some fruit to eat.

Note: Reproduce this pattern for students to color, cut out and wear.

Toucan Head Band

1. Color the headband.
2. Reproduce and cut out the pattern pieces.
3. Attach a back strip to the headband and fit to the student's head.

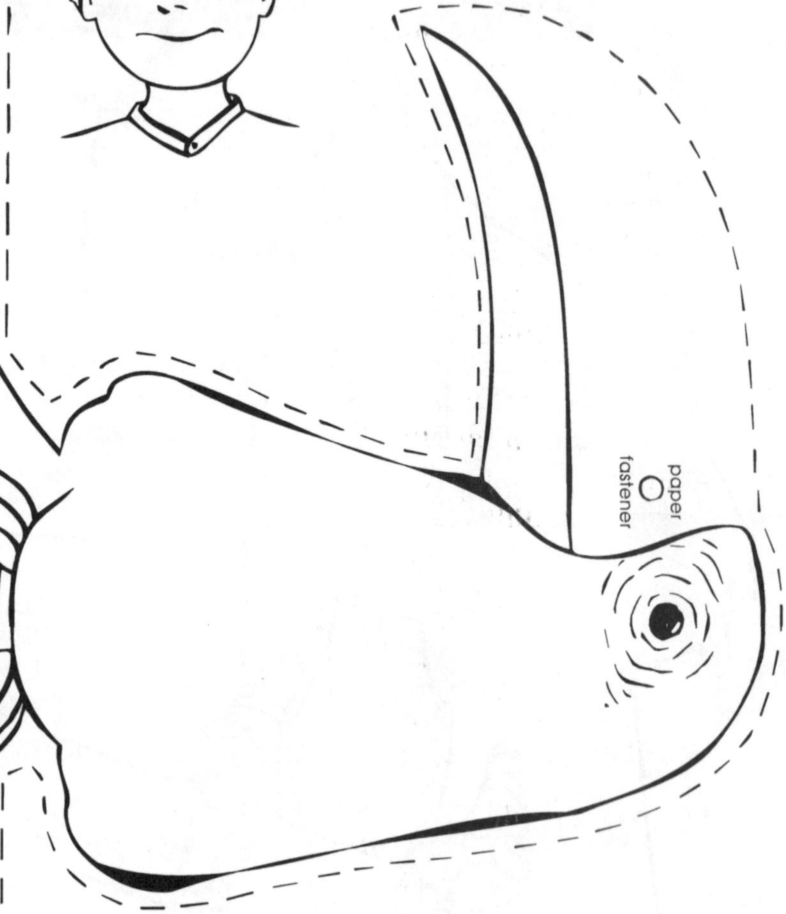

Attach the upper beak to the toucan with a paper fastener.

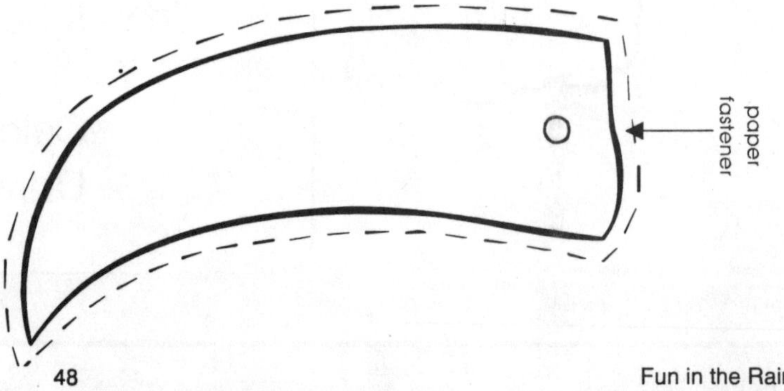